Unseen Worlds
and
Practical Aspects
of
Spiritual Discernment

By Anastacia J. Nutt, M.A.

D1738141

Unseen Worlds and Practical Aspects of Spiritual Discernment
By Anastacia J. Nutt

Published by:
R. J. Stewart Books

Copyright © 2008 Anastacia J. Nutt
Cover art by Jerry Gehringer, Boulder, Colorado

First Edition

Printed in the United States of America

A Catalogue record for this book is available from the Library of Congress.

ISBN: 978-0-9819246-0-1

R. J. Stewart Books
P.O. Box 802
Arcata, CA 95518
www.rjstewart.net

The Prayer of
the Priest & Priestess

By Anastacia J. Nutt, 1999

As I Enter the Sacred Temple of My Inner Knowing,

I Purify my Being in Preparation
for the Initiation I Have Longed to Find,
I Cleanse my Mind,
I Cleanse my Heart,

I Strip Away All That Stands Between My Forgetting
And My Remembrance,

I Make Myself Ready,

And Wait in the Knowing That It Will Come.

Table of Contents

Foreword

This book was written to encourage a paradigm shift within the spiritual and magical arts community. Through its pages, I advocate that we relinquish our use of the terms "spiritual defense" and "psychic protection." Why was it important to write a book aimed at changing these traditional terms of art? It is important because words have a great deal of power; specifically, they have the power to condition the consciousness of both the writer/speaker and of the reader/listener. Though commonly used (and therefore often not viewed in such a manner), when examined closely it is clear that terms like protection and defense set the mind in a very particular direction. When focused in the protect and defend direction, there emerges within us a desire to separate the world into dualistic categories of "good" and "evil" as these categories assist us to determine who or what we are defending or protecting ourselves against. We, the defenders and protectors, are the "good", fighting against the "evil" beings and forces we encounter. Included in our "good" category we often incorporate the terms "light" and "positive". Comparatively, within our "evil" category we often incorporate the terms "dark" and "negative". While trite categories like "good/light/positive" and "evil/dark/negative" are convenient and settling to our mind and emotions, these categories actually do not exist within the spiritual worlds in the degrees of purity and wholeness anticipated. Frankly, they do not exist within the seen world either; though many religious zealots would like us to believe otherwise. In actuality, energetic and material systems of the seen and unseen worlds are simply more complex than we might wish them to be. When we spend time looking deeper into anything we consider purely "good" or "evil" we find our simplistic categorizations do not hold up. If you have worked within unseen worlds, you know that the energetic and material spectrums are not divided into "good" and "evil" categorizations. Though there are aspects of the unseen worlds that resonate with the extreme "light" and "dark" ends, they are relatively small in comparison to the greater proportion of the spectrum which lies within the "grey" middle zone. Thus, it stands to reason that when we focus our consciousness and our resulting spiritual and magical practices on the terms "protect" and "defend" which begets our thinking in the simplistic terms of good" and "evil", we miss the greatest mass within the unseen worlds which is nominally "grey". If, instead, we direct our consciousness to relate to the larger "grey" otherworldly zones as well as the smaller "black" and "white" zones, we will greatly improve the accuracy and applicability of our spiritual and magical practices. I believe moving away from the terms "psychic protection" and "spiritual defense" to the term "spiritual discernment" is the first step toward shifting the paradigm that inadvertently encourages us to exclude the greatest proportion of the unseen worlds.

Toward this end, it is important to note that this is not an entry-level text; it is written for practitioners of spiritual and magical arts that possess an intermediate level of skill and experience. This is not to say this book will not interest or benefit a beginner, but rather to relay that many of the spiritual and esoteric terms, concepts and practices referenced within are not put forth with the explanatory language that one would normally find in an elementary text. For a newly interested practitioner this book's intermediate-level discourse may create extra work initially, but by all means partake.

Several times throughout the book, I refer to the teachings of the Path of the Ceremonial Arts (PCA). PCA is a three year community-based spiritual and ceremonial training program that my beloved Priestess partners Lila Sophia Tresemer, Katharine Roske and I co-founded in 1999. Nine years later, we employ seven facilitators, teach an average of sixty students annually, have amassed a pool of nearly one-hundred graduates and started an international program in Palestine/Israel. PCA was created to provide a temple environment within which men and women could remember and return to the sacred arts that can and should inform our lives. Our mission is simply Remember, Heal, Transform.

Through these principles, we assist men and women of spirit to remember the sacred, unite with their soul's knowing and heal through the transformative power of community ritual. As both the impetus and underpinning for this book stems from my PCA work, it is often referenced within. If you would like more information about the PCA program or our temple, The StarHouse, please visit {www.PathofTheCeremonialArts.org} and {www.TheStarHouse.org} respectively.

You may have noticed the phrase "men and women of spirit" used in the preceding paragraph. A few years ago I began using this phrase to refer to persons who devote a significant portion of their time and consciousness to improving themselves and affecting the greater good through diligent spiritual practice. Though I would prefer the terms Priest and Priestess, they still harbor a regrettable degree of misinterpretation in our culture. Please note that to me, the term "men and women of spirit" is always and in all ways synonymous with the terms Priest and Priestess.

Beyond that which is taught in PCA, the definitions and methods used in this book are based upon the Western Esoteric Tradition. I relied heavily upon the experience that my work as a Minister of The StarHouse, founder/teacher of the Path of the Ceremonial Arts and professional seer has afforded me. In addition, I resourced the writings of the following Western adepts: Rudolph Steiner, Dion Fortune, William E. Butler, William G. Gray, Paracelsus, Iamblichus and Plato. Finally, I offer special thanks and acknowledgement to the teachers, mentors and students who have shaped me: Jane Cunningham, M.A., L.P.C., David Tresemer Ph.D., Doug Jones, R.J. Stewart and the men and women of the Path of the Ceremonial Arts. I also offer special thanks to Marella Colyvas who generously contributed her editorial prowess to the final manuscript.

Anastacia J. Nutt
Spring Equinox, 2008

Introduction

During the 2005 and 2006 Path of the Ceremonial Arts (PCA) program years, the topic of psychic protection and spiritual defense surfaced on several occasions. Though this topic is fundamental to spiritual and magical work of all kinds, questions and concerns presented by PCA men and women were noticeably increasing in intensity and scope. So unusual and strong were these inquiries that I began to wonder why questions of this nature were increasing. In an effort to determine the cause, I spent some time reflecting upon the ways in which today's world has changed and the degree to which this change affects our spiritual sensibilities and therefore our spiritual practices. I also spent time speaking with our students to learn more about the nature of the spiritual concerns they harbored. During this period of reflection and investigation, I arrived at two factors or suppositions to explain why new prominence was bestowed upon the topics known to most as psychic protection and spiritual defense

The first supposition I've arrived at to explain our student's heightened concerns is based on technology. Many men and women of spirit are concerned about the impact our technologically-driven world has on their spiritual and magical practices. We wake to technology, commute via technology, work with technology, eat by technology and relate to one another through technology. Technology in the form of computers, cell phones, television, movies, video games and e-mail permeates every aspect of our lives these days. Several students I spoke to are concerned about the impact this constant technological bombardment has upon their sacred imagination, their consciousness and their relationships with otherworldly beings. In addition, many felt challenged to continually meet the needs of their mind and body in the wake of the energetic bombardment (e.g. electrical currents, microwaves, wireless internet, airport security systems, etc.) they experience in our modern, technological life.

Technology has taken hold of our world in a grand manner. As practitioners of spiritual and magical arts, we are working in vastly different conditions today than those in which our spiritual predecessors worked. Though we may be tempted by the dream of retreating away from our techno-world toward some remote and simple past, by and large, this is not the wisest soul choice for us. We must instead accept that we have chosen to be here...now; the "now" we choose is as much a part of our soul's unfolding as the spiritual and magical practices we rely upon for our growth and transformation. Instead of retreating in rejection of our current situation, we must foster new skills and abilities that enable us to meet today's new complexities with an appropriate balance of cultural acclimatization and personal forbearance.

The second supposition I've arrived at to explain our students' heightened concerns is based upon religion and spirituality. In addition to living in a new and rapidly changing technological culture, we are living in new and rapidly changing religious culture. For centuries, the religious institutions in power reigned supreme, casting judgment and life circumstance upon those they governed. The powerfully manipulative face of organized and politicized religion has long been a bane of civilized society. Religious institutions that have historically been exempted from public scrutiny are finally entering a period of closer examination. Many people are currently casting a disdainful, backward glance upon the corrupt hierarchies that so blatantly and obtrusively ruled the lives of our ancestors. This hindsight examination is urging humanity forward as a whole to reassess right relationship between religious organizations, political power, sexuality and gender. Practitioners of all faiths are being asked to dig through the rubble of the religious, social and political manipulations of the past to unearth and abide by that which is truly sacred within the roots of our faith-based convictions. Concerned for the efficacy of any ascribed spiritual or religious practice, practitioners are taking a second and third look at the ways in which spirituality is represented and practiced in their lives.

When we consider the combined impact of our technologically-driven world and religious reorientation, it becomes clearer why spiritual defense or psychic protection is on the minds of practitioners. We are in the midst of a dramatic shift in the way our world functions (technology) and the human ideologies around which much of society revolves (religion and spirituality). When shifts of this magnitude take place in the physical world, it also shifts our orientation to the beings and energies of the unseen worlds. To be clear, it's not the beings and energies of the unseen world that shift, but rather our orientation to them that shifts via the way our consciousness adapts to the worldly changes described. In light of these shifts, it makes perfect sense that practitioners of spiritual and magical arts would harbor new concerns for the associated discipline known to most as psychic protection and spiritual defense.

As is so often the case, the men and women of PCA focused my attentions in the direction where their spiritual lives needed fortification. In response, I spent considerable time researching the related esoteric teachings of the adepts of the past and reflecting upon the current world environment in writing this book. I sincerely hope it provides solid ground upon which men and women of spirit may fortify their spiritual knowledge and practices.

I would like to begin by putting forth in more detail my conjectures regarding the technological and religious changes we are facing today; after which, I will shift my use of the terms "psychic protection" and "spiritual defense" to a term more appropriate for us in today's climate: spiritual discernment.

We Are Living in a Media-Laden Time

We are all living in a time of increasing complexity on many fronts (political, religious, social and environmental.) Specialized and highly technological systems broadcast the latest news on these fronts to us all day, every day. If we spend time immersed in pictorially-based and graphic television or computer media, we are subject to a vast array of fast-paced and deeply stirring images of all kinds. Though perhaps less pictorially graphic, the messages incorporated in print and radio news are no less comprehensive in their effect. In the instantaneous click of a button, we are able to see and hear in full detail the latest mass killing, raging forest fire, pharmaceutical panacea, videotaped hostage torture or violent new computer game. All of these examples of modern media offerings contain intensely graphic, rapid-fire imagery. Imagery like this possesses the capacity to create "unlawful images" in the conscious and subconscious mind of the receiver. The concept of "unlawful images" stems from the work of Dennis Klocek, author of *The Seer's Handbook* and professor of the Consciousness Studies Program at the Rudolph Steiner College in Fair Oaks, California. In this context the term "unlawful" does not refer to civil legality; it refers to mental imagery created by external sources counter to the natural laws of the imagination. Unlawful images are energetically charged representations imprinted into our minds by an outside source; as opposed to our own internal, creative source. Further, an unlawful image is an image that is designed in such a way that we will never be able to penetrate to its archetypal being because the creator of the image was either trying to sell us something or consciously prevent us from perceiving their motive for creating the image[1]. If externally-derived unlawful images stockpile in our minds unbalanced by our own purely derived imaginative creations, the subfloor of our psyche becomes polluted with them. When this occurs, the sacred imagination we rely upon in our spiritual and magical practices becomes polluted as well. If you doubt the ability of an unlawful image to stockpile in your consciousness, bear this in mind. How easy is it for you to recall the most recent blood laden picture in the headlines of any syndicated news source you've seen? How easily can you recall a thoroughly frightening scene in any horror movie you watched in your youth? For many of us, within seconds we are able to recall the images associated with each of the preceding suggestions because they are retained within us. If unlawful images stockpile in our minds, our imagination and creativity can become stymied by the presence of these imprints which are not self derived. As time progresses, we risk becoming a physical center of attraction for additional external reflections of the prominent imagery stored in our consciousness. Put simply, we will continually draw to us reflections of the same deconstructive images and experiences that we harbor. These deconstructive images and experiences brought to us by the subtle forces of the astral plane impact our consciousness and therefore our spiritual and magical practices.

---

[1]From a conversation between Dennis Klocek and the author, November 2007.

My first point of contemplation with regard to the increased concerns of spiritual or psychic protection can be summarized as follows. We live in a time of technological and media inundation which amplifies the intensity of the world's current social, environmental, political and religious atmospheres. If we are not vigilant, we can unwittingly become storehouses for the kind of externally-derived unlawful images that negatively impact our waking and dreaming consciousness. Anything that affects our consciousness in this manner affects our spiritual and magical practices.

One might argue that our spiritual ancestors were engaged in magical and spiritual practices during similarly intense times (e.g., World War I, World War II, The Cold War) and that the realm of personal spiritual discernment is not so different for us today. I believe that the breadth and depth of deeply impacting imagery readily available to us today creates a more potentially hazardous psychic effect than that borne by our spiritual ancestors of the nineteenth and twentieth centuries. Further, instead of divorcing ourselves from the cultural impurities that concern us, I would assert we must be as innovative spiritually as the technologies that govern our lives. The matrix within which we live our lives is what it is and whether we acknowledge it or not, it adds significantly to the complexity of our spiritual and magical work.

All Religions and Practices Are Striving for Efficacy in a Scrutinizing Environment

The second understanding I came to while contemplating our community's increased interest in psychic protection and spiritual defense is related in affect, but distinct in origin. Due to the gradual liberation of our various global religious and social systems, information about the previously silhouetted alternative spiritual traditions is becoming more and more mainstream. Movies, television shows, magazine articles and bookstores now feature a plethora of "how-to" information about the magical arts (albeit with varying degrees of accuracy). In the past few years, the number of times our center has been contacted by the local press for a feature article about alternative spirituality has more than tripled. That said, I would also assert that the global culture is not necessarily more tolerant of alternative spiritual pursuits, just more curious. Commensurate with the rise in popularity of alternative spiritual practices, we are seeing a corresponding rise in fundamentalism. Both ends of the religious spectrum are experiencing a simultaneous amplification. The uncovering of unacceptable sexual conduct in the Catholic hierarchy, exposure of fraudulent accounting practices among charismatic Protestant leaders and general infighting as to the moral legality of gay and lesbian church leaders are all examples that illustrate the increased scrutiny facing mainstream religions. It seems the public is no longer willing to accept the secretive and always trusted historical status quo of religious institutions. Tired of the "we are the righteous" role that mainstream religions often play in global politics, many are determined to look elsewhere to affect positive change.

However, the increased interest in alternative spiritual paths presents as much of a challenge as it does an opportunity. Earnest persons seeking less righteously dogmatic but equally effective spiritual practices are buying spiritual "how-to" books and immediately engaging in exercises that open them to unseen worlds for which they are unprepared. Spiritual seekers are going to classes and workshops taught by persons who are themselves not grounded in a healthy lifestyle or sacred art form and yet are guiding others as spiritual teachers. Situations like these cultivate a great deal of confusion and misdirection in a time when we cannot afford either. Thus at the same time mainstream religions are facing their skeletons, alternative spiritual practices are being put to the efficacy test. Teachers and practitioners of alternative spiritual practices are being asked to prove that they can and do produce the same positive and lasting effects of the mainstream religions. I will offer an example of this efficacy test from my own work.

In 2004, Lila Sophia Tresemer and I met an Israeli peace worker and holy woman who was exhausted in her efforts to foster real change in her homeland. Her daughter-in-law was part of our women's PCA program and thus she had heard quite a bit about The StarHouse and its commitment to Sacred Union[2]. One spring morning the three of us met over cups of tea to discuss the ever intensifying situation in Israel/Palestine. Our new

---

[2]The terms Sacred Union, Sacred Marriage or Hieros Gamos refer to a concept of unity that is created by a merging of the formative opposites of the created world (e.g. male and female, sun and moon, heaven and earth). What one aspect creates alone (though exceedingly important) is not as great as that which can be created when opposites merge in co-creation.

friend asked, "Your work has noticeably helped my daughter-in-law. If I gather the women, would you offer the tools and skills of PCA to my Israeli and Palestinian friends?" Filled with an equal amount of inspiration and naiveté, we agreed to offer our program to these women of the Middle East. In accepting this offer, our hope was to catalyze the living memory of Priestess that lies beneath the cultural and religious strife these women navigate daily. Four years later, this remains the cornerstone of our work. Amidst varying degrees of failure and success, we gratefully continue our work in Palestine/Israel meeting and fostering relationships with some of the more remarkable women of the world. Though this work is challenging, our commitment remains strong because the establishment of peace in a land that so dramatically impacts us all is worth it. I am sure each practitioner perusing this book has his or her own story to tell about the ways in which their spiritual practices have pushed them into new and different territories.

Perhaps as a result of the precarious emergence of alternative spiritual traditions, mainstream and non-mainstream religious traditions are being put to the test. Whatever the impetus, it is fast becoming a time for serious, heart-dedicated spiritual persons of all theocratic persuasions to walk their talk. It is important that persons attracted to alternative spiritual traditions are as scrutinizing as their Christian, Muslim or Jewish counterparts are learning to become. Illusion and religion have a long history of entwinement; no faith or practice is exempted from this charge. Men and women of spirit must engage in their spiritual work with the same kind of caution, clarity and conviction as the Saints, Priests/Priestesses, Prophets and Saviors they emulate. We are all being asked to "rise up" to the causes we can affect in positive ways and thus find ourselves called to broader and more distant playing fields. To meet this charge, we must broaden our abilities and hone our skills of psychic protection and spiritual defense.

Conclusion and an Invitation

In contemplation of the question, "Why are men and women of spirit suddenly more interested in matters of psychic protection and spiritual defense than before?" we have explored the changes in our world which necessitate a corresponding change in our spiritual and magical practices. The change advocated through this book is a reorientation away from the terms "spiritual defense" and "psychic protection" toward the term "spiritual discernment." The material that follows this introduction is organized into two sections. The first section is titled "Foundations & Definitions:" it contains basic information relevant to the structure and orientation of the unseen worlds, their polarities and the causes and symptoms of spiritual disturbance. The second section is titled "Methods & Applications:" it contains the means through which a student of spiritual and magical arts may work to develop their own, reliable spiritual discernment practice. Throughout the book, exercises and meditations are titled and set apart as indented text in an effort to aid the reader's ability to quickly locate them after the initial read through.

To begin working with this material and creating your own practice of spiritual discernment you will need three things: time, personal commitment and a blank journal dedicated to this work. With this, I invite you to commence your journey into this discipline.

Foundations and Definitions

Though often used when referencing the subject at hand, I am purposefully not employing the phrases "spiritual defense" or "psychic protection" in this book. While learned practitioners may not be derailed by these terms, in my experience the words protection and defense propagate a particular mindset and mode of operation that misdirects our consciousness. This misdirection, in turn, informs our spiritual and magical practices. Though I doubt the intent of these statements was to misdirect us, very often they do. Sometimes the use of the terms "defend" and "protect" are espoused by well-skilled adepts mindful of their actual, historical use. More often, these terms are used by persons who lack the spiritual experience and training necessary to avoid their conditioned misuse.

I am aware of quite a few readily available modernized magical teachings[3] that by default, instruct their readers to "protect" or "defend" themselves from the hazards of the unseen worlds. As men and women of spirit, we must understand that due to the current popularization of magic and ritual, persons with inadequate levels of experience and practice are enticed to offer instruction. Such persons relay teachings that are simply a regurgitation of information they have read in the published works of the adepts[4] of previous generations while they them-

[3] In using the phrase "modernized magical teachings," I am seeking to distinguish the New Age principles and practices that naively and inappropriately introduce persons to ritual and magical practices with little to no true foundation from the "traditional magical teachings" that are based upon recognized and realized foundations (see bibliography).

[4] The word "adept" is used to describe persons who have thoroughly attained the knowledge and ability to work proficiently as spiritual and magical practitioners of the highest order.

selves possess little or no genuine personal experience. If you read the writings of the adepts of the past, you will see they often refer to aspects of spiritual and magical practices that "could not be included here" or "are topics for a deeper discussion." In some cases, these phrases pay homage to the social etiquette and publishing protocol of the time, which was more conservative than it is today. Most often these phrases pertain to the aspects of ritual practice that were historically revealed only to initiates and could not be written in books to be read by non-initiates. In other words, they refer to that which can only be revealed to persons seriously engaged in the work at hand for the greater (and not personal) good. If a modern day teacher of ritual arts restricts their expertise to a study of the written texts of the previous generation, void of deeper personal work and experience, many of the finer aspects of spiritual and magical practice are occluded from their knowledge base and thus, in turn, their instruction.

When, void of deeper understanding, we engage in "New Age" methods of psychic protection or spiritual defense that shut out, block or disband negative spiritual energies from our field of working[5], something critical to the art form is subjugated. The intention embedded within this instruction is that we learn to safeguard ourselves from negative spiritual forces and their effect. Yet in focusing our consciousness on the act of "defending" or "protecting," we can very easily make the mistake of negating all spiritual energies, thus staving off contact with the beneficial beings and energies as well as the challenging ones. In such instances, the axiom "throwing out the baby with the bath water" is apropos. This kind of misapplication is what leaves newly interested practitioners believing spiritual and magical practices do not work, when in fact it is their method that falls short, not the art form itself. I firmly believe that in matters pertaining to the unseen worlds, a warrior-like act of protecting or defending is seriously inferior to a wisdom act of filtering and discerning. Thus I have chosen the title "spiritual discernment" versus "spiritual or psychic protection" to underline the point that as men and women of spirit we must build the particular spiritual muscles

---

[5] The phrase 'field of working' is a term of art, coined by the author to represent the area within which a spiritual or magical practice occurs. It consists of the total area of conscious attention and spiritual invitation. For an individual working at a personal altar, this would consist of the space around him or her. In a larger ritual setting, this would consist of the room or location within which the ceremony occurs.

that grant us the ability to distinguish and differentiate spiritual energies. My approach is based upon the assertion that it is best to cultivate an ability to work within a magical containment in a discerning and filtered rather than a protected and defensive manner. This ability enables us to recognize and filter negative forces that can harm us while at the same time invite beneficial spiritual energies that strengthen and support us. All of the information offered in this text is built upon this initial premise. With the "discern" versus "protect/defend" modification in place, we are ready to delve deeper into the definitions and foundations of spiritual discernment. As is so often the case in spiritual and magical practices, we must begin by looking at our own part of the equation. If we are to advance in our spiritual and magical work, we must accept and abide by the fact that we are each individually responsible for our own spiritual well being. No matter how wonderful the teacher or how grand the teachings, they cannot do the work for us. We must remain awake in our spiritual and magical practices, caring for ourselves each step of the way toward a deepening of our ability and results. Thus, our study of spiritual discernment begins in earnest with a discussion of the foundation of personal responsibility that is vital to this practice. In the section that follows you will find a series of bolded statements, each of which articulates one personal, foundational principle pertinent to the practice of spiritual discernment. Following the statement are details and examples that expound upon these foundational statements. Each of these statements, and the explanations that follow, represent an aspect of personal responsibility we must assume when choosing to engage with the beings and energies of the adjacent worlds.

Only We Can Build the Spiritual Muscles That Grant Us Safe Contact with the Spirits And Beings of Adjacent Worlds

> *When we follow the dead after they have passed through the gates of death, we enter into a world inhabited by all kinds of elementary beings who are endowed with form and who really belong to that world (as we belong to this one)*[6] – Rudolph Steiner

Just beyond the boundaries of our own world, many adjacent worlds exist that operate according to their own design.

---

[6] Steiner, Rudolph. *True and False Spiritual Paths*, Rudolph Steiner Press, Dornach Switzerland, Third Edition 1985, pp. 154.

These adjacent worlds are populated with energies and beings that belong to and function within their worlds as we belong to and function within our own. As humans we dwell within the physical world; however we do not always confine our activities to that world. Our participation in particular forms of meditation, divination and ritual grants us the ability to commune with the beings and energies of adjacent worlds. Some of us go so far as to devote part of our spiritual practice to actively restoring harmony and balance between the human beings of our own world and spirit beings of adjacent worlds. In these and other ways, human beings move beyond the confines of the physical world. Similarly, the beings of adjacent worlds do not always confine their activities to their own worlds. They may also elect to surround, permeate and witness the physical world as spectators or informants for greater evolutionary purposes. Beyond these peripheral engagements, through dreams, visions and rituals beings of the unseen worlds engage with humans in an overt manner as well. In these ways, many of the interactions and roles beings of adjacent worlds assume are benevolent and helpful. However, otherworldly beings and energies can also produce spiritually or physically retarding effects upon the physical world.[7] Understanding the existence of retarding forces in adjacent worlds and preparing appropriately to avoid harmful interactions with them is an important part of the process of personal spiritual maturation. As we mature physically and emotionally, we become more and more aware of our personal responsibilities and specifically how to avoid physical and emotional dangers or stresses by being more carefully aware of ourselves. As we mature spiritually, the same is true; we must learn how to avoid spiritual dangers or stresses by being carefully responsible for ourselves. Figure 1 contains a sampling of the adjacent worlds that permeate and circumambulate the human world. Looking upon this figure, you will see many of the terms we come to regard when learning of the various beings and energies that populate all of the adjacent worlds. Note that this figure is not meant to imply hidden persuasions of rank, but instead uniqueness and distinction. Further it is to remind us humans, that we are share consciousness and space with many other beings and should thus regard our place among them as

---

[7] Ibid.

Figure 1: A Sampling of the Otherworld Relationships[8]

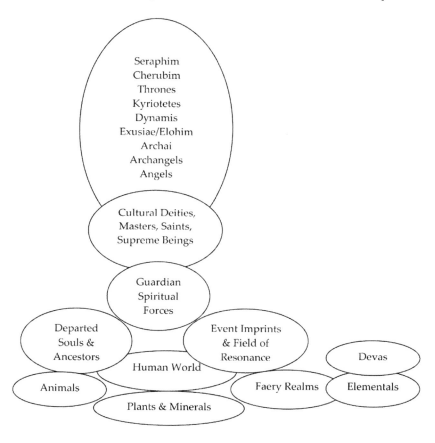

co-creative and not supreme. Toward the bottom of this figure we see the worlds that exist within and around the Earth: plants & minerals, animals, humans, faeries, elementals and devas. Just beyond these we see the world of the deceased humans, energetic imprints on place and guardian spiritual forces, of which I will soon speak at length. Beyond these, we see the beings that inspire the great religions and movements of faith of the Earth's peoples. Finally, we see the world populated by the order of beings whose domains, though increasingly cosmic, impact and influence many of the otherworlds closer held by the Earth's

---

[8]This figure and the subsequent figure on page 33 are based upon the author's experience, coupled with the anthroposophical teachings of Rudolph Steiner and Sergei O. Prokofieff and esoteric teachings of Dion Fortune.

embrace. When we realize just how complex and vast the other-worlds truly are, our understanding of Steiner's quote improves greatly by both scale and relativity. When we desire to engage with the "otherworlds" we must realize just how vast they truly are. We must also realize we humans are quite different from the life forms central to these worlds. To build our capacity for interacting with them, dormant faculties within us must be awakened. First we need to learn how to extend our gross physical senses beyond the confines of the physical world. Next we need to learn to discern the difference between healthy, beneficial engagements and unhealthy, detracting engagements.

Even though a personal trainer can effectively instruct us how to perform certain weight training exercises that improve our strength and physical fitness, we must lift the dumbbells ourselves. Only our own physical efforts will build our own body's muscles. All the expert physical fitness advice in the world will not benefit us if we fail to engage ourselves in the required acts. What's more, we cannot progress to weights beyond our muscle's capacity without risking injury. We must master the five pound dumbbells before we can safely progress to the ten pound dumbbells and beyond. These same two principles of physical fitness apply to awakening the dormant faculties that allow us to interact with the beings and energies of the other-worlds. While spiritual teachers can impart methods and techniques for assessing the appropriateness or calibration of any particular spiritual being or energy we encounter, we must diligently work to develop our own means for determining which spiritual practices, beings or energies to engage with and which to avoid. Further, we must cultivate the faculties that assist us to expand our consciousness and increase our spiritual abilities in a step-by-step fashion; skipping steps only places us at risk in the long run. In the Western Esoteric Tradition, we are responsible for our own spiritual growth. The ability to commune with the spirit world lies within each one of us; it is part of the human design. As such we must develop the inner faculties that shift our consciousness away from the limits of the mundane world and toward communion with the inner and unseen worlds.

Through the teachings and practices offered within the Western Esoteric Tradition, practitioners engage in a continual process of self-purification and transformation. This process guides each in his or her own evolution, shifting consciousness and building spiritual abilities[9]. Spiritual work requires changes of us and in turn changes us. By the very same token, adopting a practice of spiritual discernment will undoubtedly involve change; change in the way you think of and interact with unseen worlds and over time, change within you. The methods and applications referenced in this book are guideposts or trail markers toward a different condition of consciousness. While reading this book will assist you in understanding the nature of otherworldly foundations and principles, it is no substitute for engaging in the important individual work of developing your own spiritual muscles. It is my sincere request that you proceed no further in this pursuit until you have fixed your individual responsibility for your own spiritual well being in your mind and come to terms with the inevitable changes that this discipline will require of and return to you. Individual responsibility is the first and most critical factor within the seven areas of personal responsibility pertinent to the practice of spiritual discernment. In the following pages, I will discuss the remaining six areas of responsibility each practitioner must face as they begin to develop their own practice of spiritual discernment.

We Must Let Go of Any Unrealistic Fantasies and Fears We Harbor That Color Our Interpretations of the Beings and Energies We Encounter in the Unseen Worlds

When our understanding of the unseen worlds and their inhabitants is based upon youthful and inexperienced ideas, we can harbor desires and fantasies that lead us to believe that all beings and energies we encounter in adjacent worlds are benevolent in their function and intent. Likewise, when our understanding of the unseen worlds is based upon displaced fears and suspicions, we can be molded to believe all spiritual entities are malevolent in their function and intent. In either case we may suffer from our own naiveté. If naiveté such as this colors our spiritual and magical practices, we will undoubtedly make many mistakes in our assessment of the unseen worlds and their inhabitants. On one hand, we may unwittingly draw to us beings that operate upon falsely sweet premises. On the other hand, we may flee from helpful beings whose power we unjustly and ir-

---

[9]Butler, W.E. *Lords of Light: The Path of Initiation in the Western Mysteries*, Destiny Books, Rochester Vermont, 1990.

rationally fear. In both cases we are behaving in a manner that will retard our spiritual and physical well being. When we make mistakes in our appraisal of the unseen worlds we will usually experience the consequences of our error. If, for instance, we un-intentionally interact with a retarding force we may be left feel-ing energetically depleted or mildly irritated. If this interaction is prolonged, it can drain our vital forces, leaving us physically ill, emotionally unbalanced or both. When, on the other hand, we hastily dismiss a benevolent being, we may actually miss an opportunity to deepen our spiritual abilities and experiences, which would increase our capacity for greater spiritual aware-ness and, in turn, greater spiritual service. If we block the assis-tance of benevolent spiritual beings over a prolonged period of time, we can stagnate spiritually and loose touch with the poten-tial of our true spiritual capacities. Before we begin to develop a personal practice of spiritual discernment we must separate our-selves from the fantastic states of mind and emotion that keep us entangled in the mire of illusion. All this said, the concepts related to a fantastic state of mind are not necessarily black and white; thus it is important to address this subject carefully.

It is widely known and accepted that comparatively speaking, a child's state of mind offers much less resistance to the concepts of faeries, imaginary friends, spirits and angels than a typical adult's "mature" state of mind. Many books, songs and movies highlighting this contrast have been created over the centuries. Popular favorites such as Peter Pan, A Christmas Carol and Char-lie Brown portray the loss that befalls those who cut themselves off from the magical world in favor of more stable and solid "adult" pursuits. The moral presented to us adults through these tales is this: keep your child's mind alive and well so that you do not become closed to the natural magic that exists all around you. This same moral applies to spiritual and magical workings. If we enter a meditation, visualization, divination session or ritual sol-idly seated within the confines of our rational or adult mind, we will undoubtedly miss a great deal of the offering's potential. If, however we enter the same pursuits employing, in part, the as-pect of our child's mind that is open to wonder, discovery and mystery, we will experience a great deal more. That said, over the years I have met several well meaning men and women of spirit who all too quickly restrict their otherworldly experiences to those fostered by the kind of unhealthy and fantastic states of

mind that enticed them to release their rational adult-minded tendencies all too quickly.

The point I am making is this: in developing our spiritual
and magical practices, it is important to retain our child-like
willingness to experience that which we cannot judiciously explain while holding firm to our adult-minded rationalism. If we
do not balance these two aspects appropriately, we may find
ourselves navigating the two significant pitfalls into which unwary spiritual practitioners fall. When, for instance, we believe
magical fiction is a substitute for actual otherworldly contacts,
we may find ourselves navigating the pitfall of illusion. When
we allow ourselves to believe that we are the only ones that truly see the otherworlds accurately, we may find ourselves navigating the pitfall of spiritual egoism. Both of these pitfalls must
be avoided if we are to foster an effective spiritual and magical
practice that actually adds to rather than detracts from the spiritual advancement of humanity. Before addressing ways we can
monitor our illusionary and egotistical tendencies, I would like
to speak briefly to their foundations.

When we expose ourselves to too much media created to
sway and influence our actions and behaviors through the use
of fast-paced imagery, enticing advertisements and the realism
of our favorite television characters, we risk being molded by external, illusionary forces. "If you go out right now and buy this
fast car you will get the girl." "Your lover will go crazy if you
wear this perfume." "Will Jessica and Bob break up…or do they
get back together…stay tuned next week to find out what happens!" Messages like these flow across the television screen, the
air waves and printed page consistently. Enticing sources telling
us what to do, who to be and how to think are everywhere; they
include television programs, movies, video games, newspapers,
pop radio, web-based communications, popular magazines and
violent music and lyrics. Even grocery stores and banks now
feature televisions aptly placed to pacify the patrons waiting in
their service lines.

The average American is subjected to some form of enticing media presentation twelve to sixteen hours a day. We rise in
the morning and turn on the television or the radio to catch the
news and weather. Next we get into our car and drive to work
listening to a disk jockey's repartee. At work we sit in front of
a computer for eight to ten hours before jumping back into the

car to drive home...listening to the radio. Once home, we make dinner and sit in front of the television or surf the web until bedtime when we go to sleep to prepare for the same routine tomorrow. Some people actually fall asleep to the television, keeping the media vigil going well into the night. In this way, the average American is in constant contact with some form of externally-derived imaginative stimulus the majority of the day. This lifestyle leaves lunch hour, bath or shower time and sleep as the only places where quiet inward reflection replaces the external bombardment, which equates to three to eight hours a day within which the imagination has space to be purely alive. If we receive twelve to sixteen hours of externally-derived imagery a day, when we find ourselves in a quiet moment our minds will likely need to engage in a mode of stimulus integration and/or decompression as opposed to pure creation. Thus, even during these down hours we are not really offering ourselves time to think and imagine; instead we are recovering from the previous hours' media barrage.

Most of us think it is fine to live our lives constantly "plugged in" because media-based technology is pervasive in our society; it is the lifestyle many of us have known since we were children. If you were raised post 1950, it is likely that you received much of the stimulus for your creative imagination from the television and movies. Those of us who grew up being entertained by the musings of Walt Disney cannot help but associate a witch with a gnarly, haggard old woman or a faery with a cute, flying creature. Likewise, we may be so sensitized by the ubiquitous horror movies of the 1970s and 80s that we instinctively label anything with even a shade of darkness to be evil. The price of our technologically dense lifestyle comes in the form of an underdeveloped imagination and a propensity to caricaturize the world. The combination of an externally-sourced imagination and caricaturization of the otherworlds creates a precarious metaphysical foundation.

If we know we have become immersed into a technologically dense lifestyle and we wish to progress spiritually, we must perform a little spiritual housecleaning in our conscious and subconscious minds. When we decide let go of the fantasies and fears that our media-laden world has imposed upon us, we must first make the decision to studiously monitor and regulate our intake from media sources. If we do not make a decision to regulate our exposure to externally-derived images, messages and characterizations, we will continue to be a storehouse for them. And little by little, they will completely supplant our own imaginative capacity. When this occurs, the imagery and insights attained in meditation and visualization will be polluted by these external images because they're what we know.

If we wish to progress in the spiritual and magical arts, we must reclaim and maintain our sacred imagination. As men and women of spirit, a well balanced and attuned sacred imagination is a very important tool; therefore, we have to attend to its health and well being if we wish to progress in our spiritual and magical practices. The spiritual benefit received when we disassociate ourselves from externally-derived images, messages and characterizations is immense. When I unplugged myself from general media sources and unpacked the unlawful images that lay dormant within my consciousness, my spiritual and magical practices sharpened enormously. That said, disassociating from externally-derived imagery can be significantly challenging because it requires developing a discipline in what some might consider their "non-spiritual" life. Making the shift is easier once you realize that there really is no division between our "spiritual" and "non-spiritual" life. What we do, think, experience and choose in our nine-to-five, public and private life influences our spiritual work. Those who believe and operate differently are deluding themselves.

We Must Take Back Possession of Our Sacred Imagination

Our first step in taking back possession of our sacred imaginations is to regulate all new intake. This is much easier if you think of your mind's health as you do your physical body's health. Just like your body is an input sensitive entity that responds to the contents of its diet, your mind is an input sensitive organ that responds to the contents of its diet. Because this is so, it is wise to feed your mind the particularly selected "foods" that boost your spiritual intentions and aspirations rather than detract from them. I will offer an example from my own personal practice.

As mentioned above, I have phased out all routine television viewing, popular radio broadcasts and pictorially graphic news sources. Instead, I watch carefully selected television programs and movies that augment my spiritual and creative focus. I am careful not to watch violence, horror or misrepresented mythos in the entertainment I select because I know these elements catalyze feelings of separation, fear and discomfort within me which lowers my consciousness and thus detracts from my spiritual work. I am by no means cut-off from the external world; I simply choose and regulate the information to which I subject myself. I listen to National Public Radio and read the New York Times once a week for news because these sources are competent and relatively nonsensational. I read fiction, nonfiction and poetry so that I can keep the muscle of my self-derived sacred imagination strong.

Again, our first step in repossessing and eventually strengthening our sacred imagination for spiritual work is to pay attention to the intake we receive daily. We must think of our mind as we do our body by feeding it that which sustains its health and well being. As men and women of spirit we rely heavily on our sacred imagination. If we continue to allow externally-derived perceptions and interpretations of the physical and unseen worlds to become our own, we stave off the development of our own perceptions and interpretations. In this state we cannot cultivate an ability to accurately discern the nature and character of the energies and beings of the unseen worlds.

While engaging in a regime to regulate our imaginative intake, we must also steadily excavate and release the old unlawful images that linger within us. There are perhaps many ways to release unlawful images that we harbor in our imaginations. The objective is to notice the unlawful images that linger in your consciousness with enough awareness that you can recognize, locate and release them. In many situations, simply discussing and processing the images will enable us to digest and release them. In other cases, the images are deeper set and require a bit more effort. I will put forth my own method for dealing with the deeper set images.

The old, unlawful images within me usually surface in reaction to a particular state of mind or environment. If for instance I am afraid, I will sometimes spontaneously recall the imagery from an old horror movie I watched in high school. The flavor of my current experience connects me to another time when I experienced the same kind of emotional stimulation. I am sure we are all familiar with associative recall of this nature. At other times, my recall is more deliberate and comes in response to a purposeful scanning of my sacred imagination for imprints that I know need to be digested and released. If you believe you harbor fantasy or fear-based imagery in your sacred imagination (and nearly all of us do), it can be helpful to engage in a meditative clearing from time to time to first digest and then release these old images. As this is the first meditation mentioned in this book, I will offer a longer more detailed explanation of the process I have found to be helpful. In each of the meditations that follow, these introductory details will not be repeated.

Meditation to Clear the Sacred Imagination

To begin the process of recalling, digesting and releasing old, unlawful images that have stockpiled in your sacred imagination, go to your altar, light a candle and relax into a state of stillness. To enter stillness, sit completely motionless and breathe steadily for a minute or two. Now, consciously reorient your senses, one by one, away from the external world and toward your internal world. Turn your sense of sight that guides you in the external world into an inner sight that guides you through the inner realms. Turn your sense of hearing normally focused on the outside world toward the still, small voice that lives inside you. Turn your sense of touch from the dense physical body toward the delicate sensing of the subtle body. [10] *Even turn your sense of smell and taste away from the physical environment and toward the subtle realms. From here, orient yourself to the seven directions and elements that are East/Air, South/Fire, West/Water, North/Earth, Above/Cosmos, Below/Deep Earth and Within/Heart Center. Finally call to your spiritual allies who help you navigate the otherworlds. Once this foundational work is complete, we may begin the focused work of our particular purpose.*

In this quiet and intentional containment, begin to conjure the fantastic or fearful image(s) you intend to release. Allow the associations you have held with this image to be clearly and carefully understood; this is the digestion aspect of this cleanse. As you review the associations you've made between the image and your waking or dreaming life, notice how your physical or subtle body reacts to the presence of the image.

Physical or subtle body harboring of unlawful imagery is especially potent in the case of traumatic and frightful imagery. As this step can be challenging, it is best to spend a moment here. I

---

[10]The term "subtle body" used within refers to totality of the less, dense human aspects. It includes the vital/etheric body, the astral body and the mental body. The term is used in the singular sense (as opposed to subtle bodies) so as not to entice the reader to think of the subtle aspects of themselves as separate entities, but instead as interrelated parts of the whole physical body system.

would like to interject a very helpful quotation from W.E. Butler that speaks to the link I am trying to clarify.

We are far too prone to think of our mind as being in some way boxed up in our skull, though just whereabouts therein we are uncertain. But the truth is that the mind is in all parts of the body. It would be correct to say, not that the mind is in the body, but rather that the body is in the mind. The mind field extends around the body, just as the magnetic field extends around the actual steel magnet. [11] – *W.E. Butler*

The imaginative content of our consciousness is not simply filed in our brain as if indexed within a card catalog; it is stored in the body as well. If you are uncertain about this, think about the ways in which your physical body system [12] has reacted to imaginative stimulus. When I remember the death of someone I loved very much I may feel very sad or I may cry. When I recall a serious car accident I narrowly escaped in my youth, my physical body can exhibit the memories of its stress at that time. When we find an unlawful image stockpiled within our consciousness that either provokes or blocks emotion, it is likely this image resides within the body as well. To locate where images reside in our physical body system we must use and trust our intuition. Recall the image you wish to release clearly; then scan your physical body system to determine where the roots or links between the power of this image and your physical body system lie. If you are uncertain or no links with the physical body system clearly present themselves to you, you may proceed by working with the image alone.

To continue, from here, it is most helpful to engage and balance the left and right hemispheres of your brain so that all associative imprints are recalled and released during the excavation process. To do this you can simply flex and release the muscles in your fingers and toes on

---

[11] W. E. Butler. *Apprenticed to Magic: The Path to Magical Attainment*, Thoth Publications, Loughborough, Leicestershire, UK, 2002, p 49.

[12] In PCA we use the term "physical body system" in reference to the subtle relationship between the physical, etheric and astral bodies. Often emphasis is placed on distinguishing these bodies for purposes of spiritual work. In reality these bodies intertwine. The body is a whole, living system of complex and subtle interactions; thus we refer to the "system" in PCA which includes all mechanisms of the subtle bodies and the physical body.

your left and right hands and feet. Likewise you may shift you eyes back and forth from the right to the left several times. Next, return to the conjured image noticing where it lives in the physical body system. Again, realizing that this image may be stored in the sacred imagination alone or it may be stored within the subtle or physical body as well. Once recalled and clearly identified, engage your sacred imagination to determine the means by which you will physically and metaphysically encase or ensnare the image once excavated. For instance, you may envision a lasso capturing the image. Conversely, you may envision a vacuum hose sucking the image into its internal bag. Once you have determined your method of encasement, begin to see and sense the unlawful image being pulled out of your imagination and physical body system toward the encasement. A reverse spiraling motion, like the unscrewing of a light bulb out of its socket, can be helpful in this regard. Once you have fully unpacked and ensnared the image in the manner of your choosing, gather it and its encasement into your hands and offer this to the spiritual contacts that you called forth to assist you. Trust they will remove and recycle this image appropriately. Finally, purify your hands with herbs or dip them in salted water to clear them completely of the imprint. To complete the cycle you may do one or two things. You may replace the fantastic image with a blank canvas or starless sky which creates the space for new, authentic spiritual images to enter your sacred imagination when you reengage in your meditations. Conversely, you may replace the unlawful image with your own soul derived imagery sourced in the moment or from a previous meditation or working. In either case, be certain to place the space or new image into your physical body system as well.

I have found this method to be quite effective in helping me tidy up the subfloor of my consciousness. Further, I have learned (as I am sure you too will learn) that replacing unlawful images takes a fair amount of time, focus and concentration. It is, therefore, more efficient for us to avoid stockpiling these images in the first place. If you follow this course to unplug yourself from externally-derived imaginative imprints of questionable origin, you will experience a shift in the background condition of your consciousness. This shift will yield a cleaner imaginative slate upon which the sacred imagery of your choice can now be placed.

After a man has decided to abandon his wrong ways and actually does abandon them, the first task of the (spiritual) enemy is to clear a space for an unhampered field of action against him.

He succeeds in this by suggesting to the man, who has entered the right path, that he should act on his own, and not go for advice and guidance to the teachers of the righteous life...the experienced eye will at once see where he is driving and will warn his pupil. An inexperienced novice follows them (spiritual enemies) and falls into an ambush, where he is exposed to great dangers or is destroyed altogether. [13] – Lorenzo Scupoli

The preceding quotation was extracted from *Unseen Warfare*, a piece of classic spiritual literature written by Lorenzo Scupoli in the 16th century, then edited by Nicodemus of Mount Athos and revised by Theophan the Recluse. It speaks to the necessity of right guidance and alliances when one is in an earnest pursuit of mutually beneficial otherworldly relationships. If we allow ourselves to be limited by pride and the thought that we must do it alone, we are setting ourselves up for a number of avoidable mistakes that could lead us into troubled waters. Releasing unlawful images is an extremely valid and important first step in clearing any attraction we might harbor that draws to us the unhealthy forces of the unseen worlds. As helpful as this is, releasing unlawful images is largely related to what we've experienced in the past; while this is very important, it is not enough. We must also engage ourselves in such a manner that we continue to improve upon the foundations of our sacred imagination in the present. In the quote from *Unseen Warfare*, spiritual practitioners are warned against the troubles of the "go-it-alone" novice. Bound by pride, illusion and a false ego, the "go-it-alone" novice does not check or corroborate their own spiritual insights; instead they languish in the belief that they are free of any misinterpretation or misperception of the unseen worlds. Persons operating in this manner are prone to the spiritual pitfalls of illusion and false egoism referenced earlier. The pitfall of illusion threatens us when our sacred imaginations are so polluted with falsely contrived spiritual imagery that we become prone to engender thin spiritual fantasies versus deeper spiritual realities. The path to this pitfall is lined with the otherworldly fantasies and fears mentioned previously. The pitfall of false egoism threatens us when we become enticed into any

---

[13] Scupoli, Lorenzo. *Unseen Warfare: the Spiritual Combat and Path to Paradise of Lorenzo Scupoli*, edited by Nicodemus of the Holy Mountain and revised by Theophan the Recluse. St. Vladimir's Seminary Press, New York. 1978, pg. 165.

form of spiritual self-aggrandizement that isolates us from our truer, humble nature and distances us from our spiritual brothers and sisters. The path to this pitfall is lined with inflated self-perceptions, yearnings for power, misappropriated sexuality and other delusions of spiritual grandeur.

To lessen our tendencies toward the sway of illusion or our own false ego we should develop objective and subjective personal systems that allow us to cross check our spiritual inspirations and intuitions. These methods assist us when we are unsure whether or not we are seeing, sensing, hearing or feeling our own internal or otherworldly communications accurately. Objective personal cross check systems consist of the less malleable means of seeking spiritual clarity. They include the use of well founded divination tools, listening to bodily wisdom and seeking counsel from an elder or respected friend. Subjective personal cross check systems consist of more malleable means of seeking spiritual clarity. They include the use of well calibrated dream work, visualizations and meditation. Details pertinent to the discovery and use of objective and subjective cross check systems are discussed in the Methods and Applications section.

In taking back possession of our sacred imagination, we must regulate which images and impulses we allow to permeate our being because we do not simply view or hear them; we receive them into our physical body system. These images become literally entwined within us. If you still doubt this, practice the removal technique referenced in this section. Here you will see and experience just how sticky the media-driven images that permeate our lives truly are. Unlawful images of our past experiences must be supplanted by self created images that enhance rather than detract from our ability to commune with the unseen worlds. Further we must strive to balance our rational thinking and magical abilities so that we maintain a present condition that is as free from illusion and spiritual egoism as possible. When we learn to regulate intake and clear out old, unhealthy images, our sacred imagination becomes our own again. From here we can rebuild and repopulate our minds and bodies with the same beautiful, soul derived imagery that we expect to find in the finest temples and cathedrals. As physical vessels through which spiritual energies are meditated into the physical world, our minds and bodies truly are temples and as such should be tended with the utmost reverence.

We Must Understand the Nature of the Shared Substance That Binds the Worlds and How We Affect It

The adjacent worlds work on their own accord regardless of our awareness or acceptance of their existence. Our participation in ritual or meditation does not create or make manifest the unseen worlds; they are autonomous places that exist whether or not we acknowledgement them or partake of their wisdom. If we choose to engage in the kind of spiritual work that allows us to commune with the beings and energies of the unseen worlds, we should learn how these worlds both perceive and influence us.

First and foremost, the relative solidity of the physical world is a characteristic unique to that world. In the adjacent worlds, solidity is based upon an entirely different premise. I will explain this statement in a bit more detail. Things that appear solid and tangible to our human senses certify the truth of their existence. Conversely, things that we cannot see, touch and taste with our bluntly applied physical senses often pale in our estimation, becoming less true or real. The limitations of human consciousness portrayed by this contrast explain why many people do not explore life beyond the veils. Just because we do not share physical substance with the unseen world does not mean that we don't share substance. We share the energetic substance that is thought, emotion and expression, heat, light and electricity. The following quote from Rudolph Steiner will shed light on the importance of this assertion, with specific regard to thought.

> He (the student of higher knowledge) begins to deal with his thoughts as with things in space, and the moment approaches when he begins to feel that which reveals itself in the silent inward thought-work to be much higher, much more real, than the living things in space. He discovers that something living expresses itself in this thought-world. He sees that his thoughts do not merely harbor shadow-pictures, but that through them hidden beings speak to him. [14] – Rudolph Steiner, 1947

The date of this quote points out that contrary to its revolutionary portrayal in cult films like *What The Bleep* and *The Secret*, the knowledge of thought and energy as substance has been

---

[14]Steiner, Rudolph. *Knowledge of the Higher Worlds and its Attainment*, Anthroposophic Press, Inc. New York. 1947, p 30.

around for some time. The old axioms, "we are what we eat" and "we are what we think," are true. Our thoughts, emotions and physical body system's state, though perhaps not solid and tangible in form, are real and perceivable things. These subtle aspects of ourselves constitute our part of the shared substance that binds the worlds. The subtle and energetic basis of the occupants of the adjacent worlds constitutes their part. Together our subtle capacities and their subtle natures create the shared, binding substance between us.

When we emanate expansive and creative thought-forms, we literally increase the frequency of our physical body system and attract a like pulse from within the adjacent worlds. Because it is so important to our understanding the principles of spiritual discernment, let us speak to the concept of thought-form in more detail.

Thought-form is a term of art used by Dion Fortune and others to describe a product of the imagination that emanates from the mental (our thinking aspects) and astral bodies (the emotional aspects of our thinking process) of the individual outward and into the subtle and manifest worlds. Once emanated outward from its creator, the thought-form radiates a particular frequency or vibration that creates a sympathetic loop in the unseen worlds which draws back upon the creator similar, reinforcing astral and mental imprints. In this same way, a thought-form can induce similar thoughts and feelings in another person whose attentions are similarly oriented.[15] Thought-forms may be directed toward another; if they are not absorbed by that being, they will return to the creator.[16] Because our thought-forms possess the potential to become reinforced by virtue of the sympathetic laws of attraction, it is important to both create positive thought-forms that reinforce our spiritual aspirations and consciously destroy thought-forms that direct undesirable or negative aspects of the creative powers to us. When we emanate depressed or debilitating thought-forms, we attract a like pulse from adjacent worlds. In the quote that precedes this paragraph, Steiner points out that which is intangible in our world is quite tangible in the unseen worlds and vise versa. Thus whether high

---

[15]Fortune, Dion. *Applied Magic*, Weiser Books, Boston, MA/York Beach, ME, 2000. p 18.

[16]Fortune, Dion. *Psychic Self-Defense*, Weiser Books, Boston, MA/York Beach, ME, 2001. pps 197,205. [17]

or low, the frequency of our thought-forms (and physical body system, in general) is an agent of attraction or dispersion which can be perceived by others in both the seen and unseen worlds. These perceptions create affinities between "like" frequencies and repulsions between "unlike" frequencies.

Though we may be cautioned by the fact that the forces exuded by our thoughts, emotions and physical body system's state possess the power to attract or repel otherworldly beings or energies, it is important to establish that this in no way implies we should not feel angry, sad or worried. Without a vital and authentic emotional life, we are less likely to possess the potential to experience and/or facilitate meaningful spiritual experiences for ourselves and others. As men and women of spirit, not only is it impossible to fully experience our humanity without experiencing in these emotional states, it is unadvisable. Yet we must also understand that when we are in these states of being, the radiating impulses of our subtle body are affected and altered. When our subtle body is impacted, our baseline consciousness and spiritual and magical work is also impacted.

> *It signified a great deal, when in olden times whole peoples over and over again devoted themselves reverently at their festivals to the thought of their great ancestors, and united in feeling for the memory of their great forefathers. It was of extreme significance, when they inaugurated such memorial days. For it always meant the flashing up of something beautiful for the spiritual worlds.* [17] – Rudolph Steiner

When a loved one for whom we have had great affection dies, the physical attributes of his or her body are no longer available to us; however the emotional attachment we created to them is. Further, they are guided, comforted and sometimes hindered by the strength and direction of these attachments. If we wish to work successfully as men and women of spirit, we must realize this: that which is subtle in the human world manifests quite tangibly across the veils. Things that humans consider insubstantial such as feelings, thoughts and emotions are experienced quite solidly in the unseen worlds. This is why prayers and incantations work.

---

[17]Steiner, Rudolph. *The Forming of Destiny and Life after Death. Lecture 4: The connection between the spiritual and the physical worlds and how they are experienced after death.* December 7th 1915. Rudolph Steiner Archives, www.rsarchives.org.

This is why for centuries upon centuries humans have kept the custom of offering prayers and loving remembrances in honor of their dearly departed ancestors. The quote that precedes this paragraph speaks to the esoteric principle behind this custom. Our subtle (and not so subtle) communications solidify, or "flash up" as Steiner said, as they cross the borderlands between this world and the adjacent worlds.

Along these lines, it is important to discuss the perils of judgment. When we judge, or in some other manner condemn another being through our thoughts, feelings or expressive actions we close ourselves off from certain aspects of the spirit worlds. By creating these thought-forms in our imagination, we add a complementary personal imprint or signature in the unseen world. The imprints we create in the unseen world attract like beings and energies and dispel unlike beings and energies. Often when we consider the attracting principles of adjacent worlds we think of them in the positive sense: if I am good, I will attract good and dispel evil. We often do not carry the concept fully forward seeing the reverse of this principle as well. If I judge another by projecting my own aversions toward them, I am both opening myself to the same judgmental frequencies and I am repelling the gentler spiritual forces that could actually heal my heart of its discord. Judging states of mind and emotions that compel us to dismiss, hate, label or compartmentalize another person, place or thing entices us into a self-reinforcing loop. This loop both attracts the fuel it needs to stay in motion without change and dispels the healing that exists all around it waiting for an opportunity to come close. When you wonder why people embroiled in conflict cannot see how simple it is to forgive, to let go of the pain that strife-ridden clashes bring, remember this: the thought-forms within which they live and breathe are self-reinforcing. Until enough free space exists within them to open to the healing forces that exist alongside the deteriorating forces nothing can change. Let us not make the same mistakes in ourselves that we see being made in our global community. Let us, as men and women of spirit, realize and avoid the self-reinforcing loop of consciousness that a judging state of mind fosters. Mindful of the subtle capacities we possess through our thoughts, emotions and physical body system's state, we understand that it is this which binds us to the unseen worlds because the substance we share is not physical, it is energetic. As we tend to our own subtle energies (thoughts, emotions, physical body system's sate), we tend to our portion of the shared reality between ourselves and the spirits and energies whose partnerships we seek.

We Must Understand and Learn to Work Within the Polarity of the Extremes

Though spiritual and magical work can and does uplift our baseline state of consciousness over time, when we are first exposed to expanding states of consciousness we may find ourselves rising to ecstatic spiritual heights then slamming downward into the lowly spiritual depths before normalizing again. This polarity of the extremes that often meets practitioners of spiritual and magical work manifests in different forms in different individuals. I will speak of it in general terms, leaving the specifics to each individual to determine for themselves.

Our spiritual and emotional capacities do not grow in one direction, they grow in bandwidths. As we develop greater capacities to experience states of love and joy, we also develop greater capacities to experience states of loathing and despair. Likewise, as we develop greater capacities to see and perceive the higher worlds, we also develop greater capacities to see and perceive the lowly worlds. When we come out of the exalted states that are cultivated through rituals, advanced meditations and spiritual workshops we may find that we have a tendency to plummet into the depths of depression and despair. Through this cycling of spiritual highs and lows we experience the polarity of extremes. The polarity of the extremes is a phenomenon known to spiritual practitioners of all faiths; it comes with the territory of being human. It is quite complex in its make up and cannot be trivialized or standardized as it affects each of us distinctly. However uniquely it manifests within the individual, the catalyst is fairly consistent from person to person.

When humans are touched by the magic and beauty of the unseen worlds, our consciousness and our physical body system is altered. Often our heart opens and our mind expands to such degrees that the limiting habits of the personality are temporarily lifted. In these states of being we are often filled with optimism, love, hope, trust and certainty of our path in life. When we exit these states and enter back into our daily life, our consciousness and physical body system contracts. In the contraction state we may feel surprisingly pessimistic, discouraged, distrustful and in despair. The polarization of these high and low places is part of the initial rhythm and growth acclimation of a shifting and transforming state of consciousness. As we come into contact with our true and Higher Self we can feel exalted. When we then return to the current state of our being we can feel deflated. Both the highly expansive and deeply contracted states of being are short lived and are meant to offer us stones upon the path toward the greater, longer-termed transformative processes. If we were to shift dramatically and completely from our current state to a perfectly exalted state of being we would likely fracture. The spiritual guardians and inner contacts that work with us know at what pace we can evolve while staying relatively intact. If we attach too much significance to the plummet phase in the polarity of the extremes process, we can steer ourselves off course. Consciousness soars and then plummets...then, finally levels out inclusive of the benefits and insights of both extremes. This leveling out phase must be attended to with great care and prudence. The foundation for the leveling out fostered by care and prudence is found in the place where these two extremes normalize: repose and integration. So many practitioners miss this step. Instead of waiting for the lows of the post-spiritual high to normalize through rest and reflection, they move too quickly toward the next exalted spiritual experience which they feel will "fix" their lowly orientation. In doing this they secure for themselves a spiritual life that permits only the heights, no depths and no greater integration within them. Subverting the initial lows by seeking another high is a short cut and it will not bear fruit in the long run. The low places are important for our deeper transformation; they reveal our wounds, opportunities for healing, unhealthy ancestral patterns and other limiting habits of being that no longer serve us. Thus the low places within are places to embrace and not avoid. When we set aside time for integration and rest, we allow time for our consciousness to experience the heights, plummet to the depths and then gracefully and completely move upward into a normalized state of being that integrates both poles in balance. If periods of rest and integration are properly observed, over time the swings between the high and low places will become less and less extreme and our consciousness will acclimate to the new state fostered by our deeper spiritual transformation. Without this process we will likely either suffer from the polarity of the extremes or work to manipulate them by negating our experience of the lowly places.

41

Both the heights and depths are to be explored and experienced fully; and more importantly, in balance. If we do not experience both, we risk becoming too conditioned to one pole or the other; which fosters corresponding imbalances in our spiritual practices and human relationships. When we find ourselves immersed in the heights or depths, we must remember that the foundation for right action and decision making is rarely found here.

Before completing this section, I would like to offer one more observation with regard to the polarity of the extremes. Many of us have experienced the dichotomy inherent in some of the charismatic spiritual teachers of the past century whose personal lives and choices were at odds with the truly powerful spiritual teachings they imparted. Embezzlement, adultery, bigotry, drug-dependency and emotional manipulation of others are a few of the offenses perpetuated by this group of spiritually enlightened and personally challenged individuals. I believe this dichotomy can often be explained by a lack to familiarity with and/or willingness to work well within the polarity of the extremes. Confused by the incongruent spiritual and human natures of these teachers, many of their followers learned to look the other way which only served to perpetuate the problem. Though they should be appreciated for their formative aspects, the days of spiritual and personal incongruence are gone. As a human culture, we cannot avoid the challenges of the important work of an integrated self any longer. We must endeavor to cultivate and abide by personal choices that are as clean and clear outside the spiritual experience as they are inside it, striving to create uniformity between our "at the altar" and "at the office" personalities.

The practice of spiritual discernment espoused in this book assists us to tighten the relationship between our mundane and spiritual selves because it condones no separation between the two. We must all stop compartmentalizing our thoughts and deeds into boxes labeled "my spiritual self I want to share" and "my human self I want to hide." Instead, we must take full responsibility for our actions twenty-four hours a day and seven days a week because everything we think, do or say is real, in the physical world, the unseen worlds or both. When we integrate ourselves into one being, the powerful grip of the polarity of the extremes lessens a great deal. Why? Because we recognize, understand and have integrated our own human nature. Thus the extremes do not shock us or compel us into inappropriate inward or outward actions. To succeed in this endeavor, we must familiarize ourselves with the patterns of polarity that are natural to our own processes of emotional and spiritual growth. Each one of us will experience the heights and depths differently. Each one of us will require different lengths of time to acclimate back to a normalized and integrated state. Because we are all different in these capacities, it is vital that we observe ourselves in the high and low states. One primary and enduring way to accomplish this is journaling the particulars we notice in the patterns inherent to our way of experiencing these places within and without. Additionally, it is important to devise ways to arrest ourselves from taking action or making important decisions from the pole places. Whether in the exalted or deflated state, we should avoid major decisions when in them. Too many friends and colleagues have reported remorse from starting a new relationship, buying a home, spending money or quitting their jobs in these fleeting states. Sometimes we will possess the will force to stop ourselves from doing inappropriate things in these states and other times we will not. As a safety measure, I have found it quite valuable to form a bond or agreement with a trusted spiritually inclined friend, colleague or teacher. This bond gives each person permission to reach to the other when additional strength and clarity is needed while navigating the high and low places.

The State Of Our Physical Body System Affects The Quality And Capacity Of Our Work With The Spirits And Beings Of The Unseen Worlds

As previously stated, we do not share physical substance with the unseen world, yet we share substance. In that section I mentioned that the state of our physical body system draws to us and dispels from us the same spiritual beings and energies as our thoughts and emotions do. The premise behind this assertion will now be discussed. More often than not, physical manifestation in the form of an illness or imbalance presents to the vital body[18] before affecting the physical body. If the compromised vital body impulses are not recognized and addressed, the physical body

---

[18]The term "vital body" is used in this book. To be clear, the tern "etheric body" could also be used in its place throughout.

will become stressed. Because humans operate and function in a manner particular to our world we sometimes forget that our engagement with adjacent worlds changes the rules that previously governed our lives. For instance, compared to working two hours at our "day job," an equally timed magical working can impart what might seem a disproportionately level of fatigue.

It is important that we realize spiritual and magical work consumes an atypical and often greater amount of energy than the more mundane activities of our daily lives. This is partly due to the fact that we develop endurance for physical work we routinely perform, versus the spiritual work we do not. As most of us perform meditations, rituals and the like on an occasional basis, our capacity for this work is less substantiated than our capacity for our frequently performed career or family work. It is also due to the fact that we employ ourselves in one manner when we work in the physical world and an entirely different manner when working in the subtly influenced unseen worlds. To some extent we can build endurance for doing prolonged or intense spiritual and magical practices just as we have done with our work in the physical world. However, there is a limit to the degree of acclimation we can achieve. As Steiner points out, we must remember we are creatures of the physical world and the physical parameters unique to our situation. Interestingly these same parameters (e.g. time, attachment to place, hunger, etc.) do not apply in the beings of adjacent worlds. For instance, beings in adjacent worlds do not need to remember to eat, drink and go to the bathroom regularly. Because, as humans, we do have to attend to the aforementioned activities, we must cultivate a clear sense of the current limits of our physical body when we engage in spiritual and magical workings. In PCA we create what we call the *Self Care Altar*. This altar contains a lit candle, flower essences, tinctures, homeopathic remedies, vitamins, snack foods and essential oils. The *Self Care Altar* is always present when we are engaged in personal and ceremonial work. Not only does it serve to remind the physical beings in the space to take care of themselves, it is also a gesture to the unseen worlds reminding them, too, of the differences between us.

Even an experienced occultist may get into difficulties if he or she attempts magical work when in bad health, over-tired, or

has had even a moderate amount of alcohol, for very little is
too much when the Invisible Forces are being handled. [19]

– Dion Fortune

I received my bachelor's degree in the late 1980s. During those days anti-anxiety drugs were making their foray onto the general market. Stressed out, over worked and under-rested college students like me were routinely prescribed anti-anxiety drugs to help us deal with pressures of academic life. My parents saw to it that I too had my own personal antidote to stress in the form of a little blue pill. Though it was really easy to simply pop the pill each day and cruise through my courses, something deep inside me was not enthused about this choice. Thus I began to research other options to stress management. My quest led me to two books, *Feeling Good* by David D. Burns, M.D. and *Notes to Myself* by Hugh Prather. What I learned reading these books was that I could choose to stay in charge of my mental state or I may give that power away to another person, aspect or thing. Further, I could interpret my particular life situation in different ways. I could interpret the pressures of college life as stressful or creative. I could interpret my challenges as ways to become stronger versus ways I was made weaker. These realizations shifted my cognitive habits, my consciousness and consequently my need for the little blue pill. I still remember standing in front of my Persuasive Speaking 101 class with a handful of pills as I talked about the power of cognitive thought and choosing self over substance. In a dramatic moment at the end of my speech, I threw the pills into the trash can and encouraged my fellow students to do the same with their emotional crutches.

In our discourse thus far we have already established this tenet: if our consciousness is affected, our spiritual and magical practices will also be affected. If we rely on physically and emotionally altering substances as a means to escape the discovery of our own inner puzzles and patterns, our spiritual and magical work will be short circuited. In some cases we may be advised that we need a particular medication to stay emotionally and physically balanced. I am not a doctor and thus am not qualified to instruct any person as to his or her personal medical choices. In many cases, I am sure appropriate medical interven-

---

[19]Fortune, Dion. *Psychic Self-Defense,* Weiser Books, Boston, MA/York Beach, ME, 2001. p 90.

tion is necessary to help re-establish an inner balance. However, I do know that an altered state of mind, emotion or body affects us spiritually. Other spiritual practitioners also assert this truth. My personal example of over-medication is one of many that permeates our culture these days. In cases such as mine, many doctors seem to be choosing to write expensive prescriptions to pacify the imbalances of the physical body system versus expand their allopathic horizons to include traditional wisdom. Further, few if any of those dispensing them cross-reference the synergistic and antagonistic effects of combining these drugs. I know several people whose medicine cabinets are populated with pills for sleep, anxiety, depression and alertness. Who is regulating the combined effect of these pills on the physical body system?

Setting aside a truly assessed need for pharmaceutical assistance, when sincerely engaged in spiritual and magical arts, it is best to avoid unnecessary drugs, excessive alcohol, food addictions and other spiritually supplanting substances. If we routinely engage in recreational drug and alcohol intake our spiritual and magical abilities will be affected. There is no way around this truth. I and several of my colleagues who have lived through the party years of our college and post college lives all attest that our contact with the unseen worlds shifted dramatically when we let go of the consciousness altering substances of our past. If you rely upon consciousness altering substances to get by in your daily life, you will not possess the ability to cultivate certain skills and abilities that are needed to sustain a clear and consistent spiritual practice. Even if we have a reasonably well developed intuitive ability for perceiving the benefits and dangers of the unseen worlds, in a physically compromised state we are not actually able to judge with the same level of acuity. Conversely, if you do move away from any unnecessary, conscious altering substances you've used, you will undoubtedly find that your spiritual work is enhanced because the wellness and wholeness of your physical body system is enhanced. In 1995 Hawthorne Press published a wonderful book called *In Place of the Self: How Drugs Work* written by Ron Dunselman,[20] which clearly and plainly describes the spiritual alterations one can expect to experience when relying on consciousness altering substances. He also discusses the particular spiritual skills and

---

[20]Dunselman, Ron. *In Place of the Self: How Drugs Work*, Hawthorn Press, 1995.

functions that are distorted in the brain by popular recreational drugs such as marijuana, alcohol, cocaine, etc. I highly recommend Dunselman's book as you consider the points offered in this subsection.

If you have some genuine spiritual work under your belt, you know that spiritual work is demanding on the physical body. With this in mind, why would you choose to engage in activities that synthetically weaken or compromise your baseline body state? In making this assertion, I acknowledge and exempt Earth-based practices that involve the use of plant medicines in their spiritual teachings. Many persons, clearly and consistently devoted to Earth-based traditions, engage in rites of passage that utilize sacred plants in traditional ways. Plant medicine rituals attended by sanctified medicine men and women are an important part of these paths. However, the rightful use of plant medicines involves a deep commitment to the practices and traditions that subscribe to these medicines. When sacred plant medicine is utilized by spiritual shoppers who pick and choose leaving the deeper commitments and harder teachings for others, the previous warning applies.

Though We Must Be Rooted in a Healthy State of Individualism, it is Equally Important that We Realize that it is Never All About Us

All in all, the importance of esoteric order rests on much the same criteria as a teaching establishment for any discipline, from playing the banjo to differential calculus. The better the tuition the easier and better the learning – and self-tuition can be a very poor substitute, particularly in matters like ritual, where practice in teamwork is needed. [21] – Gareth Knight

I offer the preceding quotation from the distinguished Gareth Knight, Qabalist, author and co-founder of the Helios Course in the Practical Qabalah and Servants of Light as an important but often missed aspect of our spiritual and magical work. His words provide a foundation for a significant point I would like to make regarding consciousness, individuation and group work. When we realize that we are responsible for the

---

[21]Knight, Gareth. From the Forward to *Esoteric Orders and their Work* by Dion Fortune, p 10.

state of our consciousness and that it in turn informs our spiritual and magical work, a dramatic shift begins to occur in our lives. As a result of this shift, most of us will endeavor to realize and release the habitual states of being that previously bound us in cycles of victimization, self-abusive and otherwise negative modes of being. As we do this, we are able to liberate our consciousness which in turn accelerates our personal and spiritual growth. Shifts of this nature seal the leaks in our physical body system which fosters new and different expressions of self empowerment. This empowerment enables us to expand beyond the familiar, habitual patterns that have kept us stuck in disempowering modes of thought and personal expression. Freedom from the weight of our previous personal limitations is a great thing for it inspires a newly enlivened sense of individuation. However, when fully invigorated by the joys of personal liberation, some individuals lose their affinity for and their relationship to "other" and "group." These individuals become overly identified with the individuated self and forget the importance of other points of view, inclusion and diversity. We have all experienced group settings where the balance between the needs of one or two vocal individuals and needs of the collective is not well maintained.

The "I know the way...me first" mantra which often springs forth on these occasions creates an imbalance in the individual. This imbalance will also affect any group of which this individual is a member. In these circumstances one person imprisons the whole by dominating the creation and refusing to acknowledge "other" because they are caught up in the hard-won liberties of the Self. Though it is understandable how one who labors so hard to achieve actualization finds it hard to let go...let go we each must, if we are to attain an even higher degree of spiritual awareness and aptitude.

Some people believe that a strong sense of individuation is the road to true spiritual power. What they fail to realize is that in actuality, the "I know the way...me first" dynamic creates a separation of hearts and a diffusion of the true power to transform. It also orients the individual away from service to the greater (as opposed to the individual) good which must permeate all higher level spiritual and magical efforts. Self-centered mental constructs that entice us into places of separation and distinction weaken the true power within us. States of mind and heart which ensnare us into a world of ego-driven isolation are never a good thing. They are, however, a very successful means that negative/retarding forces can and do employ to keep groups from working well together and thus positively affecting change. How better to diffuse the collective power of a group of spiritual practitioners than to entice them into petty ego battles that appear to be more important than their spiritual work?

When we come into our own as men and women of spirit, it is important to do so mindful of the personal freedom and liberties of ourselves and others. As individuals we can make great strides from our places of personal empowerment, and in turn offer many gifts to our communities as fully realized men and women of spirit. However, the real magic happens when we come together in co-creation and in community. As Gareth Knight states, spiritual practitioners are engaged in matters where practice in teamwork is needed. However, few of us are taught how to co-create in our youth when such habits are initially formed. Instead we are taught to excel as an individual. The only place where co-creation is hinted at in our culture is in team sport athletics and vocal and instrumental music. Nearly everywhere else, we are encouraged to individuate, aiming to surpass the achievements of our brothers and sisters in order to succeed. To go as far as we are meant to travel as men and women of spirit, we must learn the art and craft of co-creation. Co-creative teamwork begins within us. It starts when we truly realize that though our individual freedoms and visions are important, we must tend to the balance between individual expression and the group mind, between personal freedom and co-created group attainment. If we learn to nurture our own perspective and goals while simultaneously nurturing the perspective and goals of our brothers and sisters, we will amplify the work and potential of each individual in a synergistic manner. A well founded and maintained group mind such as this increases our ability, power and spiritual protection. For those of us willing to endeavor in this manner, the amplified effect is worth the small individual compromises necessary to amalgamate the power of the individual into the power of the group.

An adept, working alone, will work a ritual in picture consciousness on the astral without moving from his meditation posture, and this ritual will be effective for the purposes of invocation...if

49

> *he wishes to raise his own consciousness beyond its normal limita-*
> *tions, transcending his own will power and unaided vision, he will*
> *make use of the powers of the group elemental developed by ritual.* [22]

– Dion Fortune

In PCA we work to cultivate an awareness that balances individualism and community via two tools, one is *The Braided Way,* and the other is *The Co-Creator's Model.* Through the use of these two tools we are endeavoring to foster a strong personal and collective foundation for the men and women who study with us. *The Braided Way* reminds us that although a strong sense of individualism is essential to our personal, spiritual foundation, its singular nature is not nearly as strong as a braid composed of our individualism, a strong circle of sisters and brothers and our cultivated spiritual and magical abilities. Through the metaphor of the braid we highlight the difference between the singular strength of an individual and the combined strength of an individual, a group and a solid set of spiritual and magical skills. To generate our ceremonies we use *The Co-Creator's Model* which consists of a set of step-by-step instructions that guide a group through the ritual planning process in a manner that honors the balance between individual contribution and group cohesion. *The Co-Creator's Model* challenges each one of us to do our part to shift the dominator paradigm we've all grown used to working within. We do this by creatively marrying the insights and inspirations of each human and spirit being drawn to co-author the particular ritual at hand in fun and exciting ways. We also make a sincere commitment to do our best to create no new personal or group shadows during the co-creation by agreeing to speak to any interpersonal blips that surface within the group as they occur. This can be challenging, but we have learned that unspoken interpersonal struggles do not simply go away; and when subjected to the transformative pressures spiritual forces tend to bring to a ritual performance, they will surface in a less desirable manner, during the ritual itself.

Before moving on, let us quickly reiterate the foundations of personal responsibility pertinent to a spiritual discernment practice. We must: 1) realize we are solely responsible for devel-

---

[22] Fortune, Dion. *Applied Magic*, Samuel Weiser, Inc. York Beach, ME, 2000, p.1.

oping our own muscles of spiritual discernment, 2) release our irrational fears and fantasies pertaining to the unseen world, 3) release unlawful images and reclaim our sacred imagination as our own, 4) learn to recognize and work well within the polarity of the extremes, 5) understand the shared substance between the physical and unseen worlds, 6) recognize and work within all of the relevant boundaries of our own physical, emotional and spiritual well being, and 7) offer our contributions to a circle in a way that balances our individualism with the power and potential of our group cohesion.

The Polarities Within the Adjacent Worlds: Negative and Positive In Action

Our acceptance of the seven points of personal responsibility made in the previous section serves as our first step in creating a practice of spiritual discernment. These seven aspects set us squarely on our feet with the proper and rational foundation that allows us to move into the craft-based and intuitive attributes of this art form. As I stated in the beginning, our goal is to *discern* and *filter* versus *defend* and *protect*. This orientation demands that we learn to distinguish the degrees of relative negativity within the unseen worlds by developing an ability to appropriately assess that which we initially perceive as negative/ retarding beings or energies. If we accept the wisdom embedded within the old saying, "we cannot judge a book by its cover," we understand that surface representations may not reveal inner content. In terms of spiritual discernment, subtle manifestations of the unseen worlds that on the surface appear either foreboding or benevolent may, in fact, not be so. I have noticed repeatedly that a simple lack of understanding in the way negative/retarding energies work causes persons engaged in spiritual and magical practices to overreact to situations they deem malicious which shuts them into a spiritually and emotionally contracted mode unnecessarily. I have also witnessed misperceptions of the opposite quality which have led men and women of spirit to stay engaged in otherworldly associations they should have flown. In this section I will briefly discuss the inherent positive and negative characteristics of the spirits and energies of adjacent worlds, giving particular attention to the negative polarity as this is most relevant to the subject at hand.

As you may know, the psyche of the human being is composed of aspects that are both positive and negative by nature; in PCA we refer to this inherent duality as our "light" and our "shadow." When we invite a new acquaintance into our lives, we may initially be attracted to the lighter and more alluring aspects of that person. In these initial engagements we also offer the lighter and more alluring qualities of ourselves. Over time our mutual acquaintance may deepen to the extent that we intentionally or inadvertently reveal our hidden or shadow aspects to each other. The power and beauty of the human being is amplified when the duality of the light and dark nature within us is accepted and unified; it is from deep within the creative tension of this polarity that our true self is birthed.

Like the human beings just described, spiritual beings and energies also embody inherent polarities consisting of the positive/light and negative/dark aspects unique to them. Perhaps you have never thought about the spirit world in this manner. If so, take a moment to think about the quality of a gentle spring rain pattering lightly upon the tender leaves of new plants just poking from beneath the ground. Now, contemplate the torrential force with which a hurricane can demolish a coastal community. In the same vein, think upon the quality exuded from a softly dancing candle flame. Conversely, call to mind the destructive power that comes to the land when lightning strikes the Earth, generating a raging forest fire that takes days and hundreds of firefighters to subdue. These two examples illustrate the creative and destructive capacity, and thus multi-faceted nature, of the elements of Water and Fire. What about the multi-faceted nature of archetypes or deities? Take a moment to recall and appreciate what you know about the delicate, feminine essence of Isis as Mother-Lover. Now shift your appreciation of Isis to her awe-inspiring power as collector and restorer of her Brother-Lover, Osiris. At the end of Act I in her poetic drama, *The Immortal Hour*, Fiona MacLeod reminds us of the multi-faceted nature of the beings of the faery realms in saying "They laugh and are glad and are terrible: when their lances shake every green reed quivers." [23]

Beings and energies of adjacent worlds are as multifaceted as we are. If we intend to work with only the gentle rain aspect

---

[23]MacLeod, Fiona. *The Immortal Hour*, Thomas B. Mosher, Portland Maine, 1907, p. 26.

of the watery West and do not distinguish these desires in calling it forth, we may unwittingly welcome the hurricane as well. The understanding and acceptance of the multi-faceted nature of adjacent worlds will greatly assist us in our spiritual endeavors. Unfortunately, many modernized magical teachings do not address this in offering spiritual instruction thus confusing and potentially derailing their students' abilities. There is nothing wrong with calling upon the wholeness of any element, energy or deity if it is chosen consciously. The goal is to know and appreciate the beings and energies of the unseen worlds such that we can readily banish that which is not desired and invoke that which is. When we understand the multi-faceted nature of the adjacent worlds and align appropriately, our spiritual and magical workings are greatly enhanced. However, when we don't understand the same, we can all too easily leap onto an uncertain path where the multi-faceted nature of the adjacent worlds challenges and unbalances us.

Not only do the beings and energies of adjacent worlds embody a uniquely multi-faceted nature befitting their essence, their purpose and effect in working with human beings will be tailored to the needs and abilities of the single practitioner or group. Each time someone asks me to tell them what to expect if they work with the Celtic God Lugh for instance, I cannot offer them a trite and tidy description of what to expect because I only know of my own capacity and experience. I do not know their inner landscape and thus cannot advise them in this circumstance. The knowledge gained by my working with Lugh is further limited by the fact that anything I would offer someone else is only accurate from a perspective of the past which says nothing about my present or future potential with this deity. Though beings and energies of adjacent worlds are often represented in a generally consistent manner in mythical literature, our own unique capacities will foster the connection that is best suited for where we are in our lives and spiritual pursuits. Though particular themes inherent to her nature will present themselves, no two persons working with Hecate will have the same exact experience. Contrary to what we might be comforted to find, there is no "go here, read this, do this and get this" methodology that can be offered to those of us interested in working with the beings and energies of the unseen worlds. We must spend time studying, opening to, meditating upon and invoking the otherworldly beings and energies of our choosing. When we apply ourselves in this way, we will learn to appreciate and work with the positive/light and negative/dark aspects of the beings and energies of adjacent worlds.

For some, the time it takes to cultivate this ability will be too much and they will opt out. But for those who take the time to properly explore the fullness inherent to the spirits and energies of the unseen worlds, a plethora of knowledge and ability will emerge within them. Just before I began teaching ceremonial arts publicly, I spent twenty-two months walking with twenty-two different goddesses in a new moon to new moon cycle. Each new moon I would create an altar to the Goddess I chose, invoke her as a spiritual mentor and walk with her for the next twenty-seven days. As the new moon approached, I would dismantle that altar and create another in honor of the Goddess I was to walk with next. Through the wax and wane of twenty-two consecutive moons, I learned to appreciate the unspeakable complexities of Medusa, Uma, Brigit, Demeter, Gaia, Hecate, Kali, Athena and all the other Goddesses with whom I walked. It was a rigorous practice to attend to while working and commuting over eleven hours a day. Yet I was sculpted and changed by each presence I encountered. The depth of understanding and veneration cultivated for these deities guides me still, nearly ten years later. By any measure, a twenty-two month investment that fosters a ten year gain is a valuable and worthy venture.

With this understanding of both the complexity inherent within otherworldly beings and energies and our need to be clear in our invocation of them, it is time to move more fully into the various aspects of the negative pole. Positive and negative energies are not homogenous in form. Just as there are varying degrees of positive spiritual energy (e.g. kindness, charity, grace, etc.) there are varying degrees of negative spiritual energy (aggression, resistance, disturbance, etc.). To aid us in our understanding of this concept, let us now explore the categorizations of negative spiritual energies and beings put forth by the adepts of the past.

All Evil Is Not Created Equal

We begin our exploration of the topic of evil by acknowledging the general nature of the otherworldly gradients, in simplistic terms, before we venture into the deeper waters of the subject. In *Figure 2: Spiritual and Otherworldly Impressions*, the broad categorizations of the unseen world are outlined. In keeping with our previous discussion regarding the multi-faceted nature of the unseen worlds, you will notice that some otherworldly beings straddle both the "benevolent" and "malevolent" categories.

Figure 2: Spiritual & Otherworldly Impressions

Highly Evolved Benevolents
seraphim, cherubim, thrones/ophanim, kyiotetes, dynamis, exusiae/elohim, archai, archangels, angels, supreme beings, masters, saints

Evolved Benevolents
angels, guides, guardian spiritual forces, faeries

Interested Benevolents
faeries, departed human imprints, ancestors of the land

Neutral Inactive
any unseen being or energy that exists but does not interact with humanity

Scavengers
filth feeders, cleaner archetypes,
destroyers who preserve life, ancestors of the land

Moderately Evolved Malevolents
trauma imprints, sticky fields, violence imprints, angry land dwellers or faeries

Highly Evolved Malevolents
demonic forces, retarding folk souls, acts motivated by Luciferic consciousness

In her book *Psychic Self-Defense*, Dion Fortune discusses the relative characteristics of four general modes within which evil spiritual forces function. Thus far in our study, we have relied upon the phrase "negative/retarding spiritual beings or energies" to describe these aspects of the unseen worlds. It is important to note that for our purposes, the terms "evil" and "negative/retarding" are interchangeable. To honor Dion Fortune's work, I will use her terms in this section; however, please realize that this is not a departure from our theme; it is instead a temporary substitution made in deference to an elder. Before we dive in to the particulars of Fortune's work, it is important to lay a foundation that distinguishes the manner in which many of us were raised to think about darkness or evil from the view she and others like her espouse.

In mainstream religious teachings, evil is a force that was created when good forces became bad forces through their own misdirection and malevolent intent. According to this outlook, the function of evil is to avert the good at any cost by seducing unwary persons into the lair and influence of evil. In the mainstream view, we are led to believe that anything possessing even a hint of negativity is evil because the demons are out to get us. Historically, within the mainstream religious system the term evil has been used so broadly as to encase the human body, nature, sexuality and women. I believe this philosophy fosters a choice-negative course, in that, those who follow it are enticed to suspect and label anything and anyone that bears the appearance of darkness as evil. The suspicious state of mind this doctrine encourages can create unhealthy patterns of separation between friends, families and communities. When I was a young girl, I attended a religious summer camp with several of my friends. I was taught there that rock and roll was evil; I was to go home and smash all of my records. Further, if my parents listened to rock and roll they would go to hell. Imagine the fear and burden I carried home believing it was up to me to save my parents. If I did not succeed in encouraging them to also destroy their records, I was told I must distance myself from them and their evil ways or risk a greater punishment in the afterlife.

Doctrines that compartmentalize the world in the black and white categorizations of "good" and "evil" affect more than our external lives. Once chosen, this line of thinking can become the basis for personal assessment as well. Individuals may divide themselves as readily as they divide the external world, thus creating a solid line which compartmentalizes their personal attributes into "good" and "evil" categories. When we divide ourselves in this manner, we tend to offer our goodness to the world around us and hide or imprison our darkness choosing a sanctified external appearance over wholeness. As enticing as this mode of operation may be, over time some part of the desire for wholeness escapes the imposed separation and things begin to fracture. At this point, otherwise devout persons will find themselves making choices that eventually reveal their hidden and disowned natures. Growing up in the Midwestern Bible belt, I attended the Methodist, Presbyterian, Latter Day Saints, Episcopalian, Catholic and Christian churches; I even went to a Baptist college. Over these long years exploring mainstream religion, I experienced the phenomenon of the disowned and disembodied darkness over and over again. As a result of the repeated hypocrisy and human fracturing I witnessed, in my early twenties I began to look for an alternative spiritual path.

With this initial discussion of the mainstream view of evil under our belts, let us move on to Dion Fortune's characterizations of evil. In the Western Esoteric Tradition, it is taught that negative/retarding energy is the natural fallout of the creation process. Like the droplets that escape a cup filling with water, energies spill out of the creative web, amass and begin to function independently. Over time, they may attract other available energies of similar resonance into their fold; this strengthens and upholds their existence. In this tradition, negative/retarding energies are viewed as byproducts of the creation process. Their origins are not maliciously aligned; rather, having fallen out of the creative process, evil spiritual forces are simply void of a completed evolutionary blueprint. That which is aligned with the cosmic, evolutionary matrix is considered "good", and that which is devoid of that alignment is chaotic and thus can become "evil." Further, evil varies by degree, purpose and affiliation. Humanity can both attract to itself resonant aspects of these energies as well as feed them via their own negative thoughts and misdeeds. As opposed to the mainstream view where we are taught we are victims of evil and thus must quickly access, judge and retreat from anything that hints of darkness, the esoteric view encourages us to learn the nuances of darkness so that we can correctly discern that which is truly malevolent from that which is simply part of the natural, destructive process of the Universe.

Without an ability to distinguish the spiritually harmful negative/retarding spirits and energies from the naturally occurring negative/retarding spirits and energies, many people mistakenly address all negativity with an equal dose of thwarting aggression or fear. On several occasions I have witnessed the debilitating effect that results from one person's misunderstanding of the difference between dark creative energies and dark harmful energies. Often this happens in the middle of a magical working. A powerful and complex spiritual force is called forth from beyond the veils; one under-skilled person erroneously assesses the presence of the creative dark spiritual forces as malevolent, swaying themselves and potentially others with their reactions. Misinterpretations such as these often can cause damage to the overall well being of the person involved as well as anyone else they seek to influence with their misplaced paranoia.

If like me, you were raised in a mainstream religion, it makes perfect sense that you should fear anything that appears dark initially. However, if we are to move deeper into our spiritual and magical work, we must undo this conditioning and look deeper. If we don't, we will plateau in our spiritual pursuits because there is a place beyond which we cannot venture unless we understand the subtleties of the unseen worlds' positive and negative characteristics. When we learn to distinguish the varying features of negative/retarding spiritual beings and energies, we will be better able to train our consciousness to recognize and avert that which we should avoid, while not overreacting to that which could assist our spiritual growth.

Developing the Ability to Distinguish Differing Degrees of Negativity

A well developed ability to distinguish varying forms of negative/retarding spiritual energies or beings is beneficial on many levels. Obviously, discerning the degrees of negativity in the unseen worlds will assist us in our spiritual and magical practices; however, the same skill will also assist us in what we might consider our mundane lives. For instance, when we walk into a home we are considering for purchase or meet a potential new friend and the quality of the energy present is fantastic, it is easy to understand what to do next: we must buy the house or engage in the friendship. However, when we encounter a negative/retarding energy in the same situation, the appropriate course of action can seem less clear. In general people are more likely to be bemused by the presence of negative/retarding energy than they are by the presence of positive/attracting energy. Positive energies and beings we understand and can more easily react to; negative energies and beings we often don't understand; thus we can be confused in determining our course. The confusion caused by the presence of negative/retarding spiritual beings and energies is caused by three primary factors: dismissal, aversion to judgment and succumbing. I will briefly outline the basis of all three factors.

Though there are some who orient toward pessimism, by and large men and women of spirit tend to orient toward optimism. Optimism is an important component of the foundation of our spiritual and magical work. If we did not believe we could shift our consciousness, co-create magic, heal our bodies or foster positive change in the world we would likely not be engaged in spiritual and magical practices to begin with. Fundamentally we know that spiritual and magical practices work best when built upon an optimistic "can do" attitude. When positively oriented practitioners are presented with something that seems contrary to the good, their tendency can be to discount it due to an internal desire to employ the "light" and deny the "dark." As opposed to taking a second look at the situation, practitioners will instead dismiss their own negative first impressions with a "Nah, this cannot be; I am overreacting…everything is probably just fine." Hasty dismissal based upon our unwillingness to accept the existence of negative/retarding spiritual beings and energies is the first factor that explains why the presence of negative beings and energies is often harder for us to discern than positive beings and energies.

The misapplication of the spiritual practice of non-judgment or non-dualism prevalent in so many spiritual traditions today is the basis of our second factor. Often practitioners who commit to practices of "non-judgment" mistakenly include "non-assessment" in their creed; however *assessment* is not *judgment*. Assessment is the discipline that all men and women of spirit we must learn to exercise when determining whether or not a particular person, activity or situation is or is not compatible with our own moral and spiritual creed. In contrast, judgment occurs when our mind contracts into a place of condemnation, which separates us from others in a negative and harmful manner. Judgment closes our hearts and limits us spiritually. Assessment informs us and guides us forward in our life. If we wish to advance spiritually, we must be willing and able to assess for ourselves that which is personally appropriate from that which is personally inappropriate. When we clearly and lovingly say "no" to something or someone, it is a choice of right alignment, not separation. I will put forth the test proposed by one of our PCA graduates when her circle reflected upon the difference between assessment and judgment. When one judges, the inner dialog usually contains externalized phrases such as "He is wrong" or "You are a jerk." When one assesses, the inner dialog usually contains internalized phrases such as "For me, this is not the right personal path" or "I don't understand his choices, so I think it is best to disengage for now." Remember this little rule of thumb the next time you find yourself grappling with this concept.

The third factor that explains why the presence of negative/ retarding spiritual beings and energies is often harder for us to discern than positive beings and energies is created by the spirits and energies themselves. Negative/retarding spiritual beings and energies temporarily entangle our ability to think clearly by casting a web around us in such a way that we become temporarily cut off from our higher faculties. Many people report experiences of confusion, apathy, weariness or frustration when in the presence of unhealthy otherworldly forms and forces. Others actually see and feel themselves surrounded in a fog or cloud of sorts. This is due, in part, to an ability negative/retarding spiritual being and energies possess to intentionally obscure their surroundings. It is also due to the mismatch of our more vital and their less vital forms; their devitalized energy fields challenge our etheric body to maintain its normal frequency.

Any one of these three factors can bind and confuse practitioners into a spiritual paralysis of sorts. Knowledge and understanding provide the way out of this paralysis. First, we must resist the temptation to dismiss our first impressions, especially when we are in new and different situations. Second, we must realize that while judgment cripples us, assessment is a vital part of our spiritual and magical practices. It is akin to the role thinning and weeding is in manifesting a bountiful vegetable garden. Third, we must remember that negative/retarding spiritual beings and energies cast fields about them that confuse and disorient human consciousness. When we feel the disarming effects of these beings and energies, we must find a way to cut the connection by immediately (and often physically) shifting our orientation to a physical place and condition of consciousness that is removed from their influence.

With the preceding discussion in place, it is time to move on to the various degrees of negative/retarding spiritual beings and energies that Dion Fortune describes in her book *Psychic Self-Defense*. The following table was created to reflect these degrees in a visually comparable format. It should be pointed out that in keeping with her disciplines and practices, Fortune describes evil in Qabalistic terms. I did my best to translate these concepts into a more general spiritual language while preserving her foundations. As we aim to understand the range and effect of the various degrees of negative/retarding spiritual energy, Fortune's descriptions are a helpful point of commencement. Before we move into this more technical description of negative/retarding energy, it is helpful to contemplate two of her simpler reflections on the subject.

We have very little exact knowledge concerning these subtle forces which are the basis of both occult attack and spiritual healing, but we have good reason to believe that in their nature they are closely analogous to electricity. They are not inanimate forces, however, but have in their nature something that is akin to life, though of a low type. It has been my experience that if we work on a blended analogy of electricity and bacteria, we get pretty near the facts; as near, at any rate, as our present state of knowledge permits. – Dion Fortune [24]

But let it be clearly conceived that the Ring "good" and the Ring "evil" are not good and evil as you understand them, but merely spinning circles of force at right angels to each other, and therefore in opposition, and it is merely the angel of the first to arise which is called "good" and the angel in opposition to the prime plane is called "evil" and it might well be that in another Cosmos the first plane would begin to spin at another angel – the angel of "evil", it would still be "good" to its Cosmos, because "good" and "evil" do not depend upon any plane or angel, but are simply relative to each other....Evil is simply that which is moving opposite to evolution.

– Dion Fortune [25]

By studying the descriptions in the following chart, you may begin to recognize and distinguish the various forms of negative/retarding or evil spiritual energy that you have encountered in your spiritual practice as well as in your waking and dreaming life. For instance, in my capacity as a ritualist, I certainly recognize the negative-positive evil principle that manifests as a sluggish chaos when those in charge of a ritual are not clear in their intentions or orientations. I also readily understand the value that the positive-negative aspects of the unseen worlds provide in their scavenging function. Negative-negative evil calls to my mind my own occasional resistance to change, manifesting in the fear or anger which often provides the fric-

---

[24]Fortune, Dion. *Psychic Self-Defense*, Weiser Books, Boston, MA/York Beach, ME, 2001. p. 186.

[25]Fortune, Dion, *The Cosmic Doctrine*, Weiser Books, Boston, MA/York Beach, ME, 2000, p. 23.

Positive Evil

Positive – Positive (highly malevolent)	**Negative – Positive (moderately malevolent)**
The principle of creative byproduct: That which is pushed out during the creative process and never balanced by the act of full manifestation. Collected and magnified over time, these by products form an independent and highly malevolent force.	The principle of chaos and unformed, substance: An infinite holding chamber where things become mired by their misdirected and unformed nature attracting life energies into immobile and ineffective patterns.

Negative Evil

Positive – Negative (scavenging)	**Negative – Negative (necessarily motivating)**
The principle of destruction: The ways in which discarded energies are consumed such that they no longer affect the evolutionary forces. (e.g. filth feeders, scavenger spirits, Kali, Pluto or Hecate).	The principle of resistance to the good: The means to choke or clog the permeation of good and benevolent forces. The friction against which the good must spring forth to ensure its ability to strive on.

tion it takes to get me rerouted toward a more productive direction. And I certainly remember my own experiences with the subculture of otherworldly evil I have encountered in my work. Before leaving your study of this table, take the time to reflect upon your own associations with these four categories of evil. As you do, journal your personal experiences with each form. From here, note as many subtle differences between the various degrees of evil or negativity as you can recall. Appreciating these four categories as they are described here is one thing; knowing them through your own past experience is quite another. If you take the time to recall your own past experiences with these four forms of evil, you will be better able to increase your capacity to distinguish these various energy forms in the future.

Of the four categorizations listed in the preceding table, positive-positive evil (the greatest degree of evil) is often the hardest for us to grasp. For this reason, I would like to spend some time discussing its origin and expression. Positive-positive evil is the byproduct of the natural formation process of Universal matter. Its initial material make-up manifested as a result of an uncompensated overflow within the process of Divine creation. If you imagine pouring milk from a carton into a cup and witnessing small drops or splashes escaping the flow, you've grasped the genesis of positive-positive evil. Once outside the creation process, these renegade material forms spin into a configuration of their own devoid of the imprints of Divine creation and evolution. Over time, this contra-Divine creation/contra-evolution configuration becomes strong enough to autonomously cast its influences upon and into the manifest world. In addition to feeding, positive-positive evil feeds upon, and is further strengthened by, the acts of humanity that carry the same energetic quality (e.g., hate, killing, war, etc.). Though positive-positive evil is a byproduct of creation that exists on its own foundational terms, it is nourished by our own human misdeeds. This co-creative concept of evil is quite different from the concept of evil put forth through the mainstream doctrines where our victimization is strongly touted and our personal responsibility negated. In the alternative case, evil exists as a natural byproduct of creation. This byproduct is fed by man's own hatred, fear and ugliness. Humans are co-creators, and not purely victims, of malevolent negative/retarding spiritual energies. Understanding this key difference will greatly assist us in developing a practice of spiritual discernment that works, truly and consistently.

W. E. Butler was another working occultist who practiced in Britain in the mid 20th century. He wrote several esoteric books and was the co-founder of the Helios Course and Servants of Light with Gareth Knight. In the last public work before his death, *Lords of Light: The Path of Initiation in the Western Mysteries*, Butler spoke plainly regarding the same aspects of evil in more modern terms which I feel may aid the reader at this point. In general, I recommend W.E. Butler because he chose to write in a way that conveyed complex esoteric instructions in a delightful and engaging manner. Like Fortune, Butler discusses evil in terms of degree. He begins his description by focusing on negative evil which he asserts is the necessary element of resistance or friction which motivates matter or energy in a forward manner. Negative evil is akin to the friction that ice on a pond grants a skater or the resistance that the dirt trail offers an uphill hiker. The negative aspect of evil is necessary and important because it is the force against which we push to move forward toward the good. He advises us not to discard negative evil as wrong or overly dark, for it is a necessary part of Divine Creation. Another kind of evil, he calls negative-negative evil, is akin to quicksand or the thick bogs from which few unwary travelers emerge. If negative-negative evil takes root within us, it can produce the kind of deep despair that could convince a person there is no hope and life is not worth living. Similar to a virus, this evil is tangible and active; when one is in the presence of negative-negative evil they will undoubtedly feel a significant energy drain or other deteriorating physical or emotional effect. From here, he speaks of positive evil.[26] Positive evil is being worked upon by a living consciousness; it is no longer the resistant or bog-like aspect of the negative and negative-negative evil, it is composed of beings and energies engaged in a deliberate and active confrontation with the will of Divine Creation. This is the kind of evil that spawns horrendous human actions such as murder, cruelty and sadism. According to Butler, positive evil creates the foundation for such historical transgressions as The Inquisition, cultural persecution and the Holocaust. When referring to these

---

[26]Note: contrary to Dion Fortune's discourse, Butler does not subdivide positive evil in his text.

particular offenses, Butler makes a very important statement in his text which I quote below.

> *(In reaction to positive evil) You can close your eyes and say, "Oh well, all these people are misguided and misdirected. It isn't really their fault, it's their upbringing and environment," but you could be very wide of the mark. There is real positive evil in the world; and, as an occultist, you'll find part of your work is putting that kind of thing right by balancing the forces. We shouldn't minimize evil when we meet it. At the same time, we shouldn't make it something terrible.* [27]
>
> – W. E. Butler

Fortune's and Butler's categorizations of evil are not as ground-breaking as they might seem to persons new to the subject of inquiry; in fact, they state as much in their books. Where might the deeper roots of this alternative understanding of evil reside? Traveling along the taproot of the Western Esoteric Tradition with this question in mind, we encounter the metaphysics of Philippus Aureolus Theophrastus Bombastus von Honenheim, otherwise known as Paracelsus. Paracelsus lived between 1493 and 1541; he was a physician, alchemist, astrologer, philosopher and mystic. To categorize Paracelsus is a difficult task for he was truly a revolutionary being during a time when holistic thinkers were scarce. A scholarly background in the Hermetic, Neo-Platonist and Pythagorean philosophies, medical training and extensive travel among the "common folk" of various countries all informed his thinking and work. In 1964, Manly P. Hall wrote and published a very helpful booklet titled *The Mystical and Medical Philosophy of Paracelsus*. Though I admit there is no substitute for studying original works, as anyone who has read sixteenth century manuscripts will attest, the writing style of the time was extremely loquacious. By distilling Paracelsus' contributions on this subject to exactness, Manly P. Hall performed a great service which benefits us in our current pursuits.

The discussions thus far have focused on what one might call the macro perspective of the cosmos as described by W.E. Butler and Dion Fortune. By turning our attention to Paracelsus, we are shifting our focus to the micro perspective of the

---

[27]Butler, W.E. *Lords of Light: The Path of Initiation in the Western Tradition.* Destiny Books, Rochester Vermont, 1990, p. 59.

individual. In promulgating his knowledge of evil, Paracelsus drew upon both his scholarly underpinnings and acquired folk wisdom. He begins his discourse by making a distinction between what he called elemental beings and elementary beings. He described elemental beings as the creatures of the invisible planes that are composed of a single element of Earth, Air, Fire or Water. Elemental beings differ from humans being in two respects: first they are composed of only one element and second, they do not possess the "alchemy of quintessence," which, according to Paracelsus, is the fifth element or the soul of man. Elementals are neither good nor bad, they simply are. They have an existence without conflict because they do not possess the stress or pressure that accompanies the compound beings (e.g., human beings). Elemental beings are an essential and vital part of the creative power of the Universe. In contrast, elementary beings are a non-essential part of the evil or destructive power within (not of) the Universe.

> *In harmony with more recent findings, Paracelsus noted that most elementaries seem to be of an evil or destructive nature. They are generated from the excesses of human thought and emotion, the corruption of character, or the degeneration of faculties and powers which should be used in other, more constructive ways.* [28] – M. P. Hall

Paracelsus understood elementary beings to be the invisible offspring of the thought-forms of human beings thus they are closely related to the imagination. When first formed, the elementary beings rely upon their creator for sustenance. They are nourished by the repeated patterns in our thoughts and emotions that originally generated their existence. If not recognized and dispelled in their infancy, these elementary beings will continue to grow, gathering both strength and force. When enough strength and force is gathered unto itself, these beings achieve a state of semi-independence from their host, which changes things significantly. At this point, elementaries attack their host and creator by inflicting mental illness, physical illness or both in such a way that the human becomes trapped in the co-creation. The host succumbs to the omnipresent en-

---

[28]Hall, Manly P. *Paracelsus: His Mystical and Medical Philosophy*, Philosophical Research Society, Los Angeles, CA. 1997, pp. 63.

tity until he or she knows no means of perception or engagement independent of its influence. According to Paracelsus, we not only become completely possessed by the evil of our own creation, we become an agent of its perpetuation. He further states that the only way these thought-forms can attach themselves to us is if we are, ourselves, a livable or fertile ground for their attachment and growth. This condition is often referenced by the other adepts as well. To summarize, if by virtue of our thoughts, feelings and inner contemplations we are receptive to any particular mechanism of evil in the world, we are vulnerable to becoming its host. Once invited in this manner, it is only a matter of time before we become another unit of force which adds to the power and worldly influence of the elementary being working through us.

In the teachings of Paracelsus we see a great deal of commonality with his twentieth century counterparts. There is, however, one key difference in his exposition on evil that is worth mentioning. Paracelsus believed that the private elementary beings created from the thought-forms of humans did not exist beyond the magnetic field of their host and creator. He believed that to survive, an elementary being must be in contact with its human parent. He asserted the physical human being gives the invisible elementary being a physical vehicle that grants it the power to act and thus affect; without this vehicle, an elementary being cannot exist. Other Western Adepts have asserted the same over time. According to Dion Fortune, a thought-form can be empowered by the intensity of its creator's continual concentration and emotional investment such that it is capable of independent existence outside the consciousness of its creator; in these cases the thought-form becomes an artificial Elemental. [29]

Journeying even further back in time, we meet the Syrian Pythagorean and Platonic philosopher, Iamblichus (circa 240 to circa 325 c.e.). He espoused a similar view over 1600 years prior to the lifetime of Fortune and Butler. He discusses his principles of creation in his treatise *De Communi Mathematica Scienta Liber* (translation: On General Mathematical Science).

---

[29]Fortune, Dion. *Applied Magic*, Weiser Books, Boston, MA/York Beach, ME, 2000, p 14.

Let it be thus for us. In the elements from which numbers (e.g. the material principle of universal construction) arise neither beauty not the good yet exist, but out of the combination of the One and the causal mater of the Many, number subsists. In these first existences [numbers], being and beauty appear, and, in turn, from the elements of lines, geometrical existence appears in which being and beauty are similarly found and in which there is nothing ugly or evil. But, in the last of things, in the fourth and fifth levels, which are composed from the last elements, evil appears...not as a guiding principle, but from something falling out and not maintaining in the natural order. [30]

– Iamblichus

Though this paragraph may appear mathematical in principle, it is in fact Universal. Unless you have read his work, you may not realize that in addition to philosophy and mathematics, Iamblichus was also a ritualist; as such he worked to preserve and further the vital awakening role that ritual plays in the evolution of the soul. Iamblichus also states ritual is the framework for the created world (good, evil and everything in between) as it is a function of the interaction of the active principles of unity and multiplicity [31]. He believed evil is a byproduct of the creative process and not a guiding principle of creation. Because of this, evil follows an entirely different organizing principle, collecting and creating matter and energy to sustain itself as would any organism falling outside an ordered structure.

In recorded terms, we will trace this falling out of the natural order explanation of evil one arm's length further along the taproot of the Western Esoteric Tradition to the Greek philosopher, Plato. Plato discusses his views on cosmology in one of his late dialogs entitled *Timaeus*. Timaeus was intended to be one part of a trilogy including *Timaeus, Critias and Hermocrates*; however it was the only dialog in this series to be completed during the last decade or so of Plato's life. In Timaeus, Plato speaks to his sense of the cosmological order of the Universe. As part of this discussion, he references the condition of the soul newly incarnated who, due to "a symptom of confusion and a cosmic order

---

[30]Shaw, Gregory. *Theurgy and the Soul: The Neoplatonism of Iamblichus*, Pennsylvania State University Press. University Park, PA. 1951. p 32.

[31]Ibid. p 33.

gone haywire,"[32] encounters evil. This evil impacts the circuits of the immortal soul descending through the creative flow in such a manner that they become altered, moving away from the "Same" and to the "Different."

> *And so at the moment we speak of, causing for the time being a strong and widespread commotion and joining with that perpetually streaming current in stirring and violently shaking the circuits of the soul, they completely hampered the revolution of the Same by flowing counter to it and stopped it from going on its way and governing; they dislocated the revolution of the Different.*[33] – Plato

Although through Plato's *Timaeus* we have followed our taproot as far back as approximately 360 BCE, it stands to reason that Plato may not be the originator of the theories of evil that exist within the foundations of the Western Esoteric Tradition. The degree to which Plato's philosophical expatiation was his own versus a culmination of his thoughts and the unrecorded thinking of his predecessors (e.g. Socrates, Parmenides or Pythagoras) is largely unknown. Though deeper roots may be found, it is sufficient for our purposes to cease our exploration here, some 2,300 years into the past, where the underpinnings of this alternate understanding of evil can be traced.

From helpful to resistant, chaotic to creative, negative/retarding spiritual beings and energies exist in various forms and thus foster various effects. When we seek communion with the spiritual beings and energies of adjacent worlds, we are entering into a potentially complex and diverse relationship. Thus it is our job as men and women of spirit to learn to distinguish the varying forms and complexities of evil that can circumvent our positive aims and desires. We cannot operate within the comfort of our own naiveté that tells us if we are "good" humans we will only attract the "good" spirits. By the same token, we must not overreact to the presence of scavenger spirits and turn into the zones of fear that siphon our creative power and subject us to more advanced forms of evil influence. In this regard, it is best to modify our spiritual and magical practices such that we clearly recognize and simulta-

---

[32]Ibid. p 9-10.

[33]Cornford, Francis M. *Plato's Cosmology The Timaeus of Plato*, Hackett Publishing Company. Indianapolis/Cambridge, Indiana. 1997. p. 148.

neously dispel the negative or malevolent forms and forces before we openly call to the benevolent forms and forces. The same logic thus far tailored to the needs and abilities of the individual also applies to the magical and ritual workings of a group. Again, I turn to Dion Fortune to underline the significance of this point; what she wrote in the late 1920s certainly applies today.

> *The uninitiated occultist goes ahead gaily, juggling with such Names of Power as he has picked up from the innumerable books on the subject now available for the general reader, thinking that if he does not invoke the demons he will not get them. He forgets that every planet (emanation or spiritual or material aspect called forth) is a Jekyll and Hyde. Consequently, ceremonial magic has gotten a bad name owing to the unpleasant frequency of untoward results. It is the imperfect technique that is the trouble.* [34] – Dion Fortune

From this point, we will be moving forward under the auspices of the alternative understanding of evil that teaches us that evil is a by product of Divine Creation influenced by contra-evolutionary chaos. Further, human beings influence and amplify, as well as succumb to, the power and presence of evil in our world. This new understanding may require you to adjust the way you have historically viewed the concepts pertinent to evil or negative/retarding spiritual beings or energies. It may also require you to adjust your spiritual and magical practices. With this basic understanding clearly in our minds, let us turn the attention toward the diagnosis or recognition of the signatures these energies leave upon us and the world of physical matter. Now that we understand all negative/retarding energy is not created equal, how do we learn to weigh and measure all that we encounter?

Recognizing Spiritual Disturbances and Their Causes

For twelve years I have been engaged in seership work, through which I commune with the spirits and energies of the unseen worlds on behalf of another. It certainly stands to reason that I started my journey with twelve years less experience than I have now. As is so often the case, I learned my way around the unseen worlds by tumbling into and being helped out of several

---

[34] Fortune, Dion. *Psychic Self-Defense*, Weiser Books, Boston MA/York Beach ME. 2001 pp 86.

spiritual potholes. Though it would be nice to be born with the wisdom of the adepts, which might grant us the ability to avoid negative experiences altogether, rarely is this the case. And as we all know, it is often our scrapes and failures that teach us the most valuable lessons in life. Whether through genuine naiveté or dim-witted arrogance, each of us tends to "place our tongue on the ice block" at some point just to see what will happen. When we do, we often require the service of a more experienced friend or benevolent inner contact to help us unstick ourselves with as little damage as possible. Often the way we recover and learn from these experiences makes or breaks our willingness to move forward in our spiritual and magical work. Hazard recognition and damage prevention is the nature of the next leg of our journey toward spiritual discernment. It is my hope that by reading this section, you will learn about some of the well known pitfalls and points of departure pertinent to the nature and constitution of the unseen worlds as well as deflect from yourself some of the hard knocks that often befall men and women of spirit.

At any point in our lives we may unwittingly be met by energies or beings that mysteriously and inexplicably immobilize, drain or sicken us. Void of any other logical, physical explanation, these ailments may herald our body's reaction to an unhealthy spiritual energy or entity. When we find ourselves devitalized due to an unhealthy otherworldly influence, we are experiencing the phenomenon known as a spiritual disturbance. In general, there are two categories of spiritual disturbances to be aware of; one is personal and the other locational. Though both affect the physical body system, personal and locational spiritual disturbances are unique in their origin. A personal spiritual disturbance originates within the physical body system of an individual and is usually due to one's exposure to a negative/retarding spiritual energy or being. A locational spiritual disturbance originates within the physical body system of a piece of land, structure or an object. It is created by a localized confluence of unhealthy or malevolent spiritual energies, beings or both. As noted, both types of spiritual disturbance affect the human physical body system. However, when we seek to remediate the disturbance, the point of focus varies between an individual or a place, space or objects. To remediate a locational spiritual disturbance, we focus our efforts on releasing or referring the unhealthy being's or energy's attachment to the site and then retuning the site to the natural, restorative powers of the primal landscape. To remediate a personal spiritual disturbance, we focus on releasing or referring the unhealthy being's or energy's attachment to the individual and then retuning the individual to the natural, restorative powers of their Divine alliances. I imagine each person reading this book has experienced some form of personal or locational spiritual disturbance over the course of their life. These disturbances are not rare, in fact, they likely occur in milder forms more often than we realize. Because this is so, when a practitioners' conversation turns toward spiritual disturbances most of us are able to contribute a few personal anecdotes and unsolved mysteries to the discussion. While the anecdotes vary from person to person and place to place, the questions that surface with regard to spiritual disturbances tend to pivot around four general aspects.

1.   How specifically do the energies and/or beings of adjacent worlds impact us and by what means can they invade our physical body system?

2.   How is it that one person engaged in a ritual working can be inordinately affected by a particular unseen force while others remain comparatively unaffected? In other words, what determines our susceptibility to the influences of the unseen worlds?

3.   If we are negatively affected by a particular otherworldly force, how do we know when it is safe to reengage in our spiritual and magical work?

4.   What is our best mode of operation against the negative and invasive forces of adjacent worlds?

The answer to each of these four frequently asked questions stems from one point of origin. Much like the concentric circles we observe when we throw a pebble into a pond; the answer to each question listed above ripples from one central point of truth. If we start there, we will discover the source of wisdom that swells forth to encompass and resolve the whole. What is the central truth of these four questions? It is the cause implied within the first question in the list: "How specifically do the energies and/or beings of adjacent worlds affect us and by what means can they invade our physical body system?" Our understanding of the difference of affect, knowing when it is safe to reengage and how to proceed when confronted by negative otherworldly forces depends upon our ability to initially connect to and thus be impacted by the energies and beings of the unseen worlds. Unless we are in some form of contact with them, the beings and energies of the unseen worlds cannot impact us. If they cannot impact us, we need not be concerned with differences of affect, reengaging or modes of operation. Thus, question one is foundational because it references the initial point of association between ourselves and the beings and energies of the unseen worlds. Once we understand the answer to this first question, we will possess the keys that answer the other three. To begin this pursuit, let us consider the following quote from Dion Fortune's *Psychic Self-Defense.*

> *There are four conditions, however, in which the veil may be rent and we may meet the Unseen. We may find ourselves in a place where these forces are concentrated. We may meet people who are handling these forces. We may ourselves go out to meet the Unseen, led by our interest in it, and get out of our depth before we know where we are; or we may fall victim to certain pathological conditions which rend the veil.* [35]
>
> – Dion Fortune

In this quote, Dion Fortune references the thin membrane that separates the seen and unseen worlds as "the veil." As discussed earlier referencing the work of Rudolph Steiner, for the most part, inhabitants of the unseen worlds live and function within their own worlds or behind their veils. However, there are many occasions when mutual observation and/or interaction occurs. This interaction is the basis of our concern; for again, without an ability to contact the other world or move beyond the veils, we would bear neither the charms nor the harms of otherworldly beings and energies. The conditions Fortune references represent four occasions when the veils separating the worlds are removed or altered to such a degree that contact is enabled between human and otherworldly beings or energies. Enfolded within these four conditions is all we need to know in our quest to answer question one above which in turn enables us to answer the remaining three. If we could put into practice the wealth of information available in Dion Fortune's quote, many of the negative impacts confronting men and women of

---

[35] Fortune, Dion. *Psychic Self-Defense*, Weiser Books, Boston, MA/York Beach, ME, 2001, p. 4.

spirit could be thwarted before experienced. Therefore, let us carefully and thoughtfully unpack each of the four conditions in turn.

Condition One

"We May Find Ourselves In A Place Where These Forces Are Concentrated."

We begin this exploration by focusing on places of concentrated or condensed spiritual and energetic force. Many such places exist throughout the world. One only needs to sit a moment and ponder all of the places where natural, spiritual or human energies tend to coagulate to get a sense of concentrated force. Churches, graveyards, battlefields, homes, temples, toxic chemical dumps, burial grounds and ancient ritual sites are all examples of places where spiritual and energetic forces may become concentrated. As you can see from the previous list, the quality of these concentrations of force ranges between the benevolent and malevolent ends of the spectrum.

> *People also come into touch with the unseen through the influence of places. Someone who is not actually psychic, but who is sufficiently sensitive to perceive the invisible forces subconsciously, may go to a place where they are concentrated at a high tension. Normally, although we move in the midst of these forces (for they sustain our universe), we are oblivious of them. Where they are concentrated, however, unless we are very dense-minded, we begin to be dimly conscious of something that is affecting us and stirring our subliminal self.* [36]
>
> – Dion Fortune

Knowingly or unknowingly, over the course of our life we may find ourselves in a location where an inordinate volume of unhealthy spiritual energy has become concentrated. When we do, our physical body system will nearly always alert us to the detrimental situation, however many practitioners of spiritual and magical arts inadvertently bypass these alerts. I will give you an example. A man of spirit decides to take a vacation to tour North American lighthouses. Nearing a particular historic lighthouse, he comes into contact with an unhealthy field

---

[36] Ibid, pp. 5.

of spiritual energy filled with imprints from the past. As he progresses deeper and deeper into this field, he notices strange feelings or sensations arising within him. For a minute, he wonders, "What is this?" However, instead of going deeper into his initial inquiry, he begins paging through the knowledge in his brain to find a logical explanation for these strange feelings. Unable to determine a truly logical cause, he simply labels himself as "out of sorts" or "silly," bypassing the spiritual explanation as too weird to ponder. In this scenario, the traveler involved instinctively *sensed* his body was reacting to something in the place, but when he *thought* about it long enough he chose to rationalize and negate versus listen to and trust his primal sensing capacity. Scenarios such as these are not uncommon. Many people miss or ignore the subtle cues their subtle body offers them. If heeded, these cues could keep them from experiencing the negativity of the unseen worlds. However, eight times out of ten, a person will rationalize the experience instead thus leaving themselves open for an unhealthy invasion. Because this mistake happens so frequently, let us explore the difference between the sensing that alerts us to an unhealthy field and the thinking that can entice us to negate it.

Our sensing capacity is different from our thinking capacity. First and foremost it utilizes a different part of our physical body system. Located primarily in our nervous system and etheric body, our sensing body receives information pertinent to the subtle changes in form and force that we encounter. In decoding the subtle changes experienced, the sensing body resources its own primal memory bank. This memory bank contains positive imprints such as love, excitement, joy, relaxation and pleasure. It also contains negative imprints such as danger, tension, trauma, caution and the like. Once detected, the sensing body offers feedback to physical body system in its own primal language. In a positive sense, this language includes, but is not limited to, warmth, relaxation of muscles, physical excitement and the like. In a negative sense it includes localized pain or discomfort, quickness of breath, dizziness, nausea and changes in bodily temperature. Because the sensing body is based in the subtle realms just beyond the physical body, it picks up on the less concrete and logical forms of information. When we enter into contact with negative/retarding spiritual beings or energies our sensing body offers us feedback of the negative character. Unfortunately, many of us ignore the more abstract language of the sensing body, choosing instead to focus on the language of our thinking capacity, which we are more inclined to understand.

Our thinking capacity is located primarily in our brain and mental body. It functions through systematizing and cataloging previous data and experiences. When we encounter a new situation, our thinking capacity seeks to reference information stored previously in our brains in determining an explanation. Because it relies on past associations, the thinking body's language is often easier for us to interpret for it is, after all, linked to a more concrete aspect of our memory. In contrast, our sensing body offers energetic impulses or signals to the brain in the form of subtle emotional and physical effects such as nausea, headache, dizziness or changes in temperature. Because these subtle messages are usually less easy to understand at first, it is easy for us to relegate them in favor of our more concrete thinking capacity.

Of course the objective in a spiritual discernment context is to combine the capacities of our sensing and thinking bodies in tandem. However, to do that most of us must spend time getting to know the language of our sensing capacity as we rely too heavily on our over-developed thinking capacity. To receive the value of the information that the sensing body has to offer, we must first understand that it is based within the primal (versus rational or logical) memory of the physical body system. The sensing body's functions are instinctual and not logical. When we understand this, it is easier for us to learn and interpret the language of our sensing capacity.

When we rely too heavily on either our sensing or thinking capacities and thus relegate one in favor of the other, we can misinterpret the situations we find ourselves in and act in a way that detracts from our overall well being. To demonstrate this principle via my own shift from an over-analytical orientation to a more balanced thinking and sensing capacity, I will offer a personal example from my work. One of my dearest and most spiritually realized friends invited me over to her new house for dinner. As soon as I walked in the door, I felt a pain in my lower abdomen and an emotional sense of pending doom. Additionally, I was repelled by an area to the right of the front door. As I walked further into the house, the feeling faded. I soon realized the house was visually lovely in every regard and I chastised myself for my initial impressions. I logically negated my sensing experience and enjoyed the evening without giving another thought to my initial impressions. About a month later, my friend contacted me in a state of despair. Her husband had been having nightmares about their new home, some quite disturbing. After investigating the previous ownerships, they learned that their home had, several years earlier, been the site of inappropriate activities that resulted in the death of several young people. The deaths occurred in the basement. Ironically, its access was immediately to the right of the front door! Through the following year, several practitioners were invited to help the family clear and re-attune their home. Eventually the painful imprints were released and the home became a loving and supportive abode for the family. Obviously my choice to relegate the messages of my sensing capacity in favor of my thinking capacity was erroneous in this instance.

A perhaps less obvious, secondary teaching is encased within this same situation which bears disclosure. I mentioned my friend was highly spiritually attuned. When we engage deeper and deeper into our spiritual and magical practices, we cultivate and carry with us unique skills and tools of otherworldly service. In this capacity we are seen as allies to the beings and energies of the unseen worlds. Thus, sometimes the intelligence of a particular place will call us to bring to it the medicine it needs to reestablish balance and harmony. When we are asked by our inner contacts and have received any other appropriate permission required, our ability and willingness to respond in such situations is part of our work as men and women of spirit. Again, I will offer an experience from my own life to augment this point.

In the late 1990s I shared a home with three friends, all of whom were engaged in creative spiritual work. At that time, one of my housemates was working on a project to honor the Dark Mother; his muse for this work was the Hebrew Goddess Lilith. When the project was complete, my friend took the statue of Lilith that had been placed upon his altar and buried it in the backyard. All housemates left the house for new horizons about a year afterward. Through a series of synchronicities, I returned to live in the house five years later. For the first several weeks, I was surprised to find myself experiencing an unusual clumsiness often tripping, stumbling and once actually falling down my spiral staircase. One morning while cleaning an altar candleholder, a large shard of glass suddenly broke free of the holder and pierced my right index finger to the bone. I spent the remainder of that morning in the emergency room. Later that day, a dear friend and colleague came to visit me. As I marveled at the continued clumsiness that finally resulted in the near extreme misfortune of almost losing a finger, she turned to me and said in an exasperated tone, "It's the house!" And in so doing, revealed the most obvious thing to the person who was shirking the truth. At once we went outside on the back patio to meditate; the name "Lil" came to my friend. Then suddenly I remembered the Dark Mother project, the statue and the burial that occurred five years before. I walked into the house and asked "Lilith, it is you?" A jar of pencils crashed to the floor in response, and thus began our ritual to remove the buried but not released imprint of this Goddess. Being the only person still around who knew of the work done previously with Lilith, I was the one who could help her with her release. After the ritual, I phone the coordinator of our Journey of the Feminine archetypal studies program, wondering if Lilith was on the roster for that year. Interestingly, she was to be invoked on the following Monday night! The spiritual intelligence that is Lilith knew she would again be summoned on this land and thus sought her release from the prior invocation. I learned a great deal from this lesson and have since honored the subtle messages of my sensing body much more astutely. If I ever forget, I need only look to the scar on my right index figure to be reminded. Once you become sensitized to and grounded within a practice of spiritual discernment, you may be drawn to places where your sensitivities and abilities can be employed to assist in the reestablishment of harmony and balance. With these examples in mind let us progress to the nature of a personal or locational spiritual disturbance.

Though each one of us is unique in our sensitivities, there are several general warning signs that indicate a spiritual disturbance is occurring. Listed below are some symptoms typical to the presence of either a locational or personal spiritual disturbance. Please note that although the Fortune quote that begins this section addresses place specifically, by and large, symptoms that manifest in locational spiritual disturbances are the same as those that manifest in personal spiritual disturbances. In both situations symptoms may be either felt acutely or they may build over time. Though this list is by no means all inclusive, the following physical and emotional effects provide a practical basis from which one can begin to assess the recognizable tone and character of a spiritual disturbance.

- Persistent localized bodily discomfort not explainable by any other physical or emotional causes or catalysts.
- Persistent mood changes not normal to the individual such as irritability, sadness, feelings of impending doom or fear not otherwise explained.
- Reoccurring and enticing dreams that seem to lock one into a desire to sleep beyond the normal requirements for rest.
- Reoccurring nightmares peppered with threatening or burdening themes.
- Sudden and unexplained loss of appetite or physical vitality, not explained by other obvious physical catalysts.
- Sudden and unexplained occurrence of heightened sensitivities to sounds, smells, light/dark and the presence of others.

When we encounter a spiritual disturbance, it is our responsibility to acknowledge and react appropriately to the otherworldly imprint with a balance of our sensing and thinking capacities. For the majority, the thinking capacity is better developed; thus it is the sensing capacity that requires attention to bring to two into balance. To begin, we must learn to pay attention to and not relegate the sensing body. The opposite of relegation is respect. When we respect the impulses of the sensing body, we not only increase our capacity to detect subtle changes in the unseen worlds, we increase our receptivity to the subtle messages offered by our inner contacts. When we have a well developed partnership between our sensing and thinking capacity, we are better able to receive, interpret and then dialog with our unseen allies. Thus, we are prone to making better spiritual discernment decisions. If you have trouble bridging your own sensing and thinking capacities there is a system I've used that may be of some assistance.

When my sensing body detects a ripple in the unseen world that may offer a particular challenge for me, I tend to experience one of the warning signs listed previously. Upon receiving this sign, I know I must still myself and take no further action until I understand what is occurring around me. In the first few moments following my sensing body's communication, I quietly create around me a safe containment and open to my inner contacts. I ask them to reveal to me the invisible energetic pattern of the current situation, gathering, person, place, etc. This specific request allows me to drop in to a direct mode of contact wherein my sensing and thinking capacities are put into a collaborative relationship with my allies in the unseen world. My sensing body extends into the space, opening to more information. My thinking body takes in the data and also listens for the direct input of my unseen allies. From here, I am better equipped to understand the most prudent next steps. I have used this particular method for several years and find it to work unfailingly.

Many of the adepts of the past warned their students against living their lives consistently open to the unseen world while absently unaware of the dense, physical world. Though the marvel and peace often found through our otherworldly communions is wonderful, if we are not equally attuned to the peace and beauty of the physical world, we will gradually create an imbalance between our incarnated and eternal selves. Over the years I have witnessed many people who erroneously think that the goal of human existence is to become "enlightened" and divorce themselves from the physical world. Though I am not a practitioner of eastern spirituality from which the term originates, I believe enlightenment is meant to create human consciousness that is fully awake and spiritually alive within the physical incarnation. In this manner we can successfully and meaningfully mediate spiritual power into the physical world creating balance between all adjacent worlds. I do not believe enlightenment, at its core, is a means of inadvertently demonizing the human form and physical world. When we default to escapist, spiritual thinking and action, imbalances manifest between our physical and subtle bodies. Imbalances of this nature can, and often do, lead to severe, life-altering consequences. First and foremost, human beings must be human. We must take care of the mundane substance of our lives in balance with the esoteric. When we sharpen our sensing and thinking partnership, we create a spiritual capacity that with time and attention becomes more and more positively habitual. With a healthy and balanced sensing and thinking capacity resting firmly within us, we are better able to live a relatively normal life, going and doing as any human being would in a consistent course of worldly and otherworldly interactions.

There is one additional observation of the first condition of engagement I would like you to contemplate before moving on. As men and women of spirit, we know the importance of attuning our personal homes and sacred spaces to embody and reflect a balanced and harmonious weaving of benevolent seen and unseen forces. If well maintained, these spaces will do a lot to automatically filter negative/retarding spiritual energies and beings for us. Vigorously tended and attended temples, such as The StarHouse, are some of the most pristine man-made places in existence today. Because they are so well cared for, fleeting lower level scavenging forces are usually the most extreme forms of negative/retarding spiritual beings and energies we experience there. Perhaps you, too, work in a sacred space or home that is well built, attuned and maintained. In such cases, one would think we should feel pleased and relieved in our creative accomplishment; however a cautionary note applies in these cases. Though we certainly benefit from working in well tuned spaces which dispel undesirable spiritual forces for us, if we restrict our working to these places, our skills and abilities will become underutilized and thus too dependent upon the "home court" forces to function. As with any acquired skill or knowledge, if we don't use it, we lose it. That which is true of mathematics or a foreign language, for instance, is also true of spiritual discernment. As with any crutch, if we use it too long, we can become dependent upon its assistance. If our spiritual discernment skills become reliant upon the pristine places within which we normally conduct our spiritual work, when we find ourselves in another location we may not possess the ability to clearly discern the unseen. If you doubt the efficacy of this warning, think for a minute on the widely documented home court advantage known in team athletics. Physically and psychologically humans become accustomed to our normal working and living environments. Spiritually the same is true, especially if you work to specifically attune your environment. If you believe you may have become too accustomed to your home or community temple, make the effort to venture into other settings by taking a spiritual field trip. In doing so any lassitude you've unwittingly developed within your normal spiritual routine or practice will be revealed to you.

I highly recommend occasional spiritual field trips as they help us keep the skills and tools of our personal spiritual discernment practice honed. I will offer another personal example to underscore the importance of this point.

Several years ago, PCA decided to venture off the mountain and rent a space in town where we could offer the Samhain normally performed at The StarHouse. In our mountainous region, snowy weather had often been a factor for this late October event. Being quite wed to our own temple, we were unsure where to look for a replacement venue. As it happened, one of our senior ministers worked in a local church that he thought might be a good site for the event. Based upon his recommendation we visited the site briefly and committed to the rental.

Though a practitioner may possess the ability or desire to do so, it is never appropriate to override the spiritual imprint or tradition of a space or place that we do not steward. Thus, as we set our sacred space that Samhain, we were careful to honor the current and intended use of the sanctuary. Once the altars were set, we built a bridge of sorts inviting the spiritual forces of our temple to join us in this space without inappropriately overlaying the spiritual orientation of the sanctuary. Though we did our best to create an appropriate container for the ritual, it quickly became clear to us that this church was not built or attuned to contain the spiritual energies of Samhain. Specifically, it lacked the attunement which would both invite the helpful ancestors and deflect the unhelpful ancestors that Samhain attracts. Throughout the event, the power of the ritual was continuously circumvented by the incompatible attunements of the sanctuary and Samhain. Over and over again, the ceremonial currents would rise and then topple. As I mentioned earlier, when we are fortunate to be bruised and not seriously injured by them, our spiritual failures present some of the best and most thorough means of learning. Our choice to use a local church for our Samhain ritual offered an important lesson. Just because a space or place has a spiritual attunement does not mean it can support any and all spiritual events. Had our selection committee actually meditated in the sanctuary, communing with the guardians of the space to assess our mutual compatibility, they would have realized the site would not work for our Samhain ritual.

In summary, though it is important for us to attune our homes, centers and temples to complement our spiritual and magical practices, we cannot afford to take shelter there and thus allow our spiritual discernment abilities to weaken. At some point, we will work in other places and spaces. In preparation for this shift, we must constantly maintain and employ our spiritual discernment muscles so that when we leave our well attuned spaces we do not become the victims of our own idleness and dependency.

Condition Two

"We May Meet People Who Are Handling These Forces."

The key to Fortune's second condition of engagement centers on right relationship. Over the course of our years in spiritual and magical practice, we will undoubtedly come in contact with other practitioners engaged in similar work. We may be fortunate to meet people who offer a deep and abiding friendship that supports and strengthens our spiritual pursuits. Conversely, we may encounter people who partake in unhealthy or ethically skewed spiritual practices. If we engage in esoteric partnerships with persons who are not centered in a healthy spiritual practice, it can detract from and even endanger our well being. This additional quote from Dion Fortune's Psychic Self-Defense really says it all.

> *The two things necessary for safety in occultism are right motives and right associates.* [37] – Dion Fortune

Over the years I have heard many stories of spiritual malpractice from friends and students. It is disheartening to realize that some people who purport spiritually advanced knowledge do not actually possess it. It is beyond disheartening to realize that to some, spirituality is a front for a business of falsehood and manipulation. When we engage in any new spiritual endeavor, be it a personal practice, group meditation meeting or community ritual, it is up to us to determine whether or not the purpose and the people are in alignment with our path and our best interests *before* we engage.

I remember one occasion in particular when I was surprised to have to make this personal assessment. I was once invited to attend a community ritual in a nearby town. As I arrived, I

[37] Fortune, Dion. *Psychic Self-Defense*, Weiser Books, Boston, MA/York Beach, ME, 2001, p. 91.

was immediately aware of a sense of chaos in the room. Walking around to gauge the situation, I passed by the center altar which was pulsing a frequency of energy so strong that I could feel it against my skin. Soon after, I noticed a man offering free energetic clearings for attendees. Obviously under-skilled in his profession, this man swept cleared energy from each person he attended into the space and in some cases directly on top of the heads of other attendees seated nearby. Turning away from my observation of this man's spiritual faux pas, I opened my inner faculties to perceive the spiritual imprint in the rest of the room. Through this meditative assessment, it became clear to me that different people were there for vastly different reasons. Some people came to party and to be seen in a social manner, some came to do community ritual in a spiritual manner and others followed the crowd with no true intention to be there at all. The altar, which was actually quite well attuned, was working hard to push the chaotic energy away from its center, thus creating the wave I felt. My sensing capacity felt the altar and the chaos in the room while my thinking capacity engaged with my inner contacts. After my inquiry, I realized this was not the environment within which I could open myself spiritually, I politely made my excuses to the friends I had come with and left.

As men and women of spirit, we are always responsible for assessing the personal integrity of any person(s) we engage with on a spiritual basis. As mentioned before, our tendencies toward seeing the good, striving to release judgment and being clouded by the influence of negative/retarding spiritual energies can sway us toward alignments that we should avoid. When we find ourselves wondering about right relationship between ourselves and another, we should exercise our skills of spiritual discernment by utilizing our sensing and thinking capacities cooperatively. Listed below are three specific questions that can assist us in our assessment of the spiritual fit between ourselves and another person, group, place or spiritual practice. When using questions and practices such as those recommended here, remember to record the situation, your inquiry and your ultimate choices in your journal. A written record of spiritual situations, deliberations, feelings and decisions is a valuable tool for future reference. Not only does a written record of this sort chronicle the concrete facts we assess and actions we take, it captures any subconscious tendencies we might harbor as well. Though this line of questioning has been a constant practice for several years now, I am continually surprised at my sensing and thinking capacity's combined ability to immediately and accurately gauge right spiritual actions.

1. How does my sensing capacity respond to a potential engagement with this person, group or practice? *If I feel drained or devitalized in any way, I may need to reexamine this engagement.*

2. What does my thinking capacity know of this person's, group's or practice's spiritual ethics and foundations? *If I know nothing, I have too little information to make my decision; I must learn more.*

3. Am I experiencing any distinguishable red lights or roadblocks as I consider this engagement (e.g. phone calls are not returned, e-mails vanish without a trace, I write the wrong meeting date in my calendar, etc.)? If so, *I may need to reexamine this engagement.*

Why do questions one and three end with the italicized phrase "I may need to reexamine this?" Because sometimes spiritual red lights or roadblocks are not guiding us to cease and desist, but are instead spiritual tests working to determine how dedicated and focused we truly are. As any experienced man or woman of spirit will attest, sometimes uncomfortable feelings and strange signals with regard to a new spiritual alignment indicate a need for us to cease our actions and other times uncomfortable feelings are a function of the kind of negative resistance that entices us forward in a beneficial manner. It is for this reason that I used the term "reexamine" in questions one and three. As I have said previously, few things governing the course between the seen and unseen worlds are black and white; most are shades of grey that we must learn to clearly distinguish if we are to function safely and effectively within our spiritual and magical practices. Accordingly, we must learn how to distinguish the "stop" messages from the "this is a test" messages accurately. If you experience strange feelings and occurrences when entertaining (or continuing) a spiritual alignment with any particular person, group or practice, it is best to reexamine the question to engage or not engage with the fullness of these two questions: "Is this signaling an unhealthy alignment?" and "Am I in resistance to or being challenged by positive change?"

Because these two inquiries can be challenging ones to work with, I would like offer a technique that assists me when I am trying to determine my own right action in cases such as these. This discernment technique was inspired by a basic method of body wisdom offered to me eleven years ago by one of my first personal and ceremonial mentors, Jane Cunningham, M.A., L.P.C., of Boulder, Colorado. Jane's many years working with body centered psychotherapy, sacred dance, Tantra and ritual have granted her a unique ability to work with a body's sensing and thinking capacities in concert. The technique explained here is based on the foundations I learned from Jane coupled with my own spiritual discernment workings; I call it *The Body Barometer*. Body wisdom is an undervalued and underutilized skill in the West, as we tend to favor our logical, thinking selves. When we learn to turn into, versus away from, our body's natural wisdom, much of the confusion related to the "Is this signaling an unhealthy alignment" or "Am I in resistance to or being challenged by positive change?" will lift.

The Body Barometer Meditation

Find the time and space to be alone for at least twenty minutes at your altar. Guide your body and mind into a meditative stillness. Light a candle, cast your working sphere and call upon your inner contacts to assist you in filtering out any distracting internal or external chatter that could taint the accuracy of your inquiry. From here, scan your body to find one place where your greatest sense of well being and physical comfort lies at this time (e.g., your heart, left foot or third eye). For today, this is your wisdom center and represents the internal elder that reminds you of your deepest and most exalted inner knowing. Note your wisdom center may always be the same place within you or it may move around depending upon the day. Thus, it is always good to scan your body in search of this place each time you use this technique. After you have determined your wisdom center, conjure up a detailed, mental image of the alliance or engagement at issue. Using your sacred imagination, go directly to your wisdom center and ask the question, "With my highest good as truth, what meets me if I do X?" Relying on the way your intuitive self functions (e.g. seeing, hearing, feeling/sensing or knowing) take note of the reaction generated within your body's wisdom center in response to the inquiry.

Here is an example of how this works. I am a seer, so I will normally receive a visual image from my wisdom center in reaction to the ques-

tion posed. Often for me, the image of a bright flower basking in the sun's radiance is my "yes/good" answer, while a flower wilting and depleted is my "no/caution" answer.

To continue, once you have received this initial response, clear your physical body system by taking several steady breaths as you mentally release the responses offered by your wisdom center. Then once again conjure up a detailed, mental image of the alliance or engagement at issue, taking care to employ the same exact detail you did previously. Ask the question, "With my highest good as truth, what meets me if I do not do X?" Again, relying on your own particular means of sensing the subtle, take note of the reactions generated within your body's wisdom center. Do not overtly engage your thinking capacity in analyzing the wisdom center's messages. Instead, trusting the body, your intuitive faculties and your first impressions; make your decision accordingly.

At this point, you will have received two distinct messages with regard to doing and not doing X which should provide the comparative and contrasting information you need to make your decision. *The Body Barometer* must be used with caution and only when you are certain of your capability to release all prior conceptions. This particular method will fail if you are in any way oriented toward the pitfalls of illusion and false spiritual egoism mentioned previously. However if used consistently, you will find that the strength of this repeatedly exercised spiritual muscle will begin to lift the allure of the pitfalls as well. All caveats in place, when considering a new spiritual alliance be it a teacher, teaching or spiritual partnership, it can be very helpful to perform this work for yourself.

Abiding by the adage, "An ounce of prevention is worth a pound of cure," it is always easiest and best to thoroughly assess new spiritual engagements *before* we step into them. After we are engaged, the damage is much more difficult to eliminate in a graceful manner. We do not have to enter into alliances if we feel uncomfortable about the alignment. Likewise, we do not have to belligerently push ourselves ahead of our comfort zones to advance spiritually. Sometimes it can simply be a matter of timing; another time the same spiritual option would be better for us than it is in the present. If we lack the personal trust and ability to clearly say "no, thank you" to a new or continued spiritual engagement, we can hurt ourselves. As a final point in this discussion please take these next unfortunate statements to heart. It is best to be aware of and able to assess our own sense of spiritual well being such that right alignments are made and wrong alignments avoided. People who are skilled in the art of spiritual manipulation look for persons who have weak boundaries, a lack of discernment and an overly compassionate orientation. You do yourself no favors by being the kind of spiritual seeker that is easily steered off course by outside influences.

Condition Three

"We May Ourselves Go Out To Meet The Unseen, Led By Our Interest In It, And Get Out Of Our Depth Before We Know Where We Are"

This third condition of engagement speaks to the perils we may face when enthusiasm and curiosity circumvent knowledge and experience. Sometimes the force of our human ego encourages us to jump head first into unfamiliar spiritual depths before we have acquired the skills and abilities to navigate these places. We may, for instance, invoke Kali, Durga or The Morrigan before we have cultivated an ability to work with these powerful forces of destruction and regeneration. We may perhaps travel to a foreign country to do intense spiritual work in a tradition that is new to us, believing we don't need any prior training in the basis of the traditional or culture. These two examples offer an illustration of the kind of arrogant spiritualism that can cause persons to step beyond their current knowledge and experience due to a lack of humility or an inflated sense of self. However, ego is not always the reason why a person would be enticed to venture far ahead of their skills and abilities.

For many of us, the spiritual journey is initially catalyzed through some form of unexpected quickening. A friend invites us to attend a moon ceremony and we become inexplicably emotional as shadowy memories of sitting in ritual circles flood our heart and mind. We may plan a vacation to Greece to relax in the warmth enjoying the calamari and ouzo. Upon a casual visit to a nearby sacred site we are awakened to a plethora of memories of temple life. Or we cautiously open the door of an esoteric bookstore and find ourselves drawn to materials we somehow remember, but no longer know. Over the past several years teaching ceremonial arts, I have come to realize that many men and women drawn to spiritual and magical work are *remember-*

ing their spirituality and not *becoming* spiritual. These memories may entice us to move toward the familiar faster than we should. So, though arrogance or ego can be the catalyst enticing some to venture beyond their depth, many are simply recalling and too hastily following their own deeply seated cellular memory.

Most of us carry memories within us that, when stirred, inform us we have been here before. These memories are keys to portals; if worked with steadily they can help us recover past work and abilities which provide a deeper foundation for our present day spiritual and magical practices. However, sometimes these memories become confused with readily available or retained abilities. Though our abilities of prior times can be reintroduced to us in this life, rarely do they arrive in such a way that includes an automatic acclimation to our current life condition and physical body system. Because this is so, we must be sure to cautiously exercise any remembered abilities in simple situations before putting them to the bigger tests. In this way we can avoid the natural enticement that arises during times of quickening that inspire us to move forward as quickly as possible to meet the yearning or memory we have excavated. Even if we were able to recall a great deal of our prior abilities in such a way that our physical body system could immediately acclimate, that was then and this is now. For reasons previously expressed, the 21st century is qualitatively different than any other time in history or prehistory. We are alive and practicing now. We must therefore learn how to engage our spiritual and magical faculties for this time and release our sentimental attachments to prior times and situations.

Though our visions caress the horizons behind and before us, we must always assess the position of our feet. To avoid wading out of our depth in our spiritual and magical practices, it is important to build and maintain particular spiritual muscles. If after living a predominantly sedentary life, we join a gym and begin curling thirty pound and pressing one hundred pound weights on the first day, we will strain and likely injure our body. To build a strong, balanced physical body without injury, we must start with smaller weights and build to the heavier weights as our muscles develop an ability to handle the strain. Our magical and spiritual practices are no different. To build a strong, balanced spiritual practice, we have to proceed step by step from the start, building a solid foundation and avoiding any enticing shortcuts. When we work in a program or a group setting, we are able to build capacity under the supervision of experienced practitioners. True spiritual mentors are monumentally helpful in matters of capacity and pace. When we practice on our own, it is important that we take care to build capacity and prepare ourselves under the tutelage of our own careful discipline. Whether working in a group or on our own, we are ultimately responsible for our own well being.

How do we know when we have moved beyond our capacity? Unfortunately many of us find ourselves in spiritually deep water before we realize it; as you may know, this can be a very sobering experience. However, we don't have to wait to find ourselves in deep water before we turn toward the shore. Not everything about the metaphysical world is mysterious and complex; in many regards we need only rely on simple *common* sense. If, for instance, you have just learned the art of purification of sacred space, you should not attempt to clear a notoriously haunted house. Likewise, if you are tired and depleted from an intense time at work, you aren't the person to volunteer to lead all night ritual chanting. So first and foremost, we must employ common, cautionary sense when we assess whether to engage and how deep to venture; this will assist us at least seventy percent of the time. Here is a good common sense rule of thumb: if the particular spiritual opportunity possesses the potential for a personal risk that could cause hardship beyond that which you are up to bearing, then it is best to walk away from the opportunity. Again, an ounce of prevention is worth a pound of cure. The remaining thirty percent of our experiences will take place within the spiritually complex and precarious grey zones. When operating in these zones, we must rely upon our spiritual discernment tools such as those already mentioned and those to come.

In both the common sense and grey zone arenas, our ability to accurately assess our own right actions is enhanced considerably if we understand and appreciate the connection between the dense physical and the vital or etheric body. The following quotation extracted from W.E. Butler's book *Apprenticed to Magic: The Path to Magical Attainment* will assist in laying the foundation for this understanding:

> *In the vital body, the life forces circulate in their appropriate channels. But the vital body is not built of ordinary physical*

matter as is the grosser vehicle we use during our earthly life. The vital body is composed of a finer type of substance, and is the dividing line between dense matter and the subtle matter of the Inner Planes. It is, in fact, sometimes known as the "linking-body," since it forms a link between the physical and the more subtle types of matter. Upon it, the physical body is built and all the processes of life in the material body depend upon the vital forces which are challenged by it. In the vital body are the connecting points which link the two levels of the physical and the so-called "astral." The vital body carries not only the life-currents of the physical body, but also that it forms the bridge between the physical brain-consciousness and the types of consciousness of the Inner Planes. [38] – W.E. Butler

It is a good idea to stop and read this wealthy quotation once more for it contains vital information pertinent to every spiritual practitioner. Without an understanding of its contents, our abilities cannot come to their full potential, so please read it again.

In the preceding paragraph, W.E. Butler speaks to the vital body and as such refers to the etheric body specifically; however our other subtle aspects (i.e. astral body, mental body) also interact with the subtle planes as was previously discussed in our introduction to the term thought-form. As repeatedly referenced, the subtle body is normally the first part of our physical body system to detect disturbances within the adjacent worlds with which we come into contact. In Butler's quote, the link between the vital or etheric body and the dense physical body is stated to be the means by which the bridges are built between us and the subtle forces of the unseen worlds. Aligning Butler's assertion with Paracelsus' assertion of the same, that which impacts the vital body will, over time, become the blueprint for the physical body. Relating back to the topic of negative/retarding spiritual forces and energies, if we spend time cultivating a relationship to the language of our subtle body, we will be able to detect the presence of challenging otherworldly imprints before they have an opportunity to become part of the blueprint of our physical bodies. With this understanding in place, let us now discuss how we can assess our work in the spiritual grey zones

---

[38] W. E. Butler. *Apprenticed to Magic: The Path to Magical Attainment*, Thoth Publications, Loughborough, Leicestershire, UK, 2002, p 42.

during the previously referenced "remaining thirty-percent of the time."

Spiritual grey zones are places of subtle distinction where simple tests of pure rationality and common sense may not be as effective in helping us to clearly discern hazardous from hospitable waters. When we find ourselves in situations where spiritual right action is less clear, our subtle body and sacred imagination are again our first allies. As we enter spiritual areas beyond our depth, our unseen allies will alert us to the dangers via their ability to influence the energetic currents of our subtle body. Most often in these situations, either a warning message is sent to the brain via the cognitive channels or an electrical signal will be received by the subtle body. As has been stated several times, to advance spiritually, we must learn the language of our own particular subtle body. If you are not familiar with the way your subtle body detects danger, three options are available to you; you may 1) make the time to learn the language of your subtle body, 2) cease spiritual and magical work because it is too demanding, or 3) forge ahead learning via your mistakes in the school of hard knocks. Many of us learn the warning signs of our subtle body the hard way; we miss its signals and bear the physical, emotional or spiritual brunt of the mistake. Obviously learning via the hard knocks is not the preferred means of acquiring spiritual experience and know how.

Though this is by no means an exhaustive list, here are a few of the signals of the subtle body that I and other practitioners I know have experienced when we have neared or gone beyond our depth. Each statement is written to reflect the practitioner's own personal experience. By glancing through this list, you may be able to retrace some of your own steps, remembering times when you, too, carelessly crossed the boundaries of your own ability and experience.

- "I noticed a gradual progression of nausea or light headedness. I had to sit down, so I knew something was off."

- "I heard/sensed a faint inner voice that warned me to stop what I was doing. I assumed it was simply my fear and pushed on."

- "A strange and unidentifiable sense of doom or danger permeated my emotions; I became a bit frightened."

- "I suddenly felt I had no idea what was happening in the room; I felt uncertain of the ritual's purpose and progression."
- "I become short of breath and very parched, as if I had just run a race."
- "My hands and feet became suddenly cold to the touch... then the rest of my physical body became remarkably cold as well."
- "I received a clear and direct message from one of my inner contacts to leave this place...and of course, to my chagrin, I disregarded it."

Your own past (present or future) warning signs may mirror the statements on this list or they may be different. Regardless, read them again paying attention to the quality of the statements as opposed to the exact detail.

Qualitatively, signs of distress come in the form of exaggerated atmospheric changes, sudden emotional shifts and changes, warning messages from inner contacts and reactions within the physical body system. Remember, for the most part the initial warnings are received by the subtle body, through subtle shifts and changes, and the sacred imagination, through meditation. If these initial signals are not heeded, the dense physical body will most likely become impacted as the distressing energies bypass the subtle bodies and begin to impact the physical body.

Though some of us receive immediate, direct and clear warning messages from our inner contacts, this is not the case for all of us. As it is so vitally important to spiritual discernment work, I would like to offer a means by which one may begin learning the language of their subtle body system. At the forefront I would like to state that during this meditation, you will be opening the closets of your memory to recall one to three times in your life when you remember being hurt, frightened or vulnerable to danger. Do not choose your most terrifying memory at the start. There is no need to trigger unnecessary trauma when discerning the way your subtle body works. Instead, pick a memory you can recall without experiencing undue stress.

Subtle Body Communication Meditation

Secure thirty minutes of uninterrupted time at your altar. Once here, move into a state of meditative stillness. Light a candle, center yourself within a sacred sphere and call to your unseen allies. State aloud your intention to come into a clear and deep relationship with your subtle body system. Choose a memory within which you felt frightened or in danger in some way. Spend a few moments recalling each moment of the incident as if you were watching a movie on your television. Don't simply play the memory forward one time from start to finish, spend time going forward and backward a few times through the memory. While doing the forward and backward play, pay attention to your current physical body system's reactions to the memory. Investigate this memory carefully, with all your senses engaged, discern if there were any hints, clues or signals that surfaced or were displayed within your subtle body prior to the crest of the incident. Be awake to all sensations, phrases, feelings or synchronicities that you notice within you now as you revisit this memory.

With regard to this revisited memory, write down all that you recalled from the past and noticed today in your journal. Gently release yourself from this memory exploration and return to stillness for several minutes. From here reengage your waking consciousness. Next, determine as many of the messages offered by your subtle body during the build up to the incident as you can, recording each message in your journal. At this point, choose another incident in your life when you remember being hurt, frightened or vulnerable to danger. Follow the same procedure you did for the first memory. When you finish recording all of the subtle body messages that you can recall, compare the two incidents to determine if there are any consistent subtle body signals between them. To close, speak a spontaneous prayer within which you express your willingness to commit to memory the language of your subtle body as revealed to you today. This prayer gives permission to your subtle body to speak, your dense physical body permission to listen and your inner contacts permission to intervene. When this is done you may release your inner contacts, open your containment, extinguish the candle and leave your altar.

To add clarity to the subtle body language learning process, I will offer a personal example from one of my own meditations. When I was ten years old I ran into a clump of pampas grass and ended up with an inch long stick wedged in my knee one day before I was to run in the state track meet. I remember hearing "be careful" from within my body and feeling particularly edgy that day as I played with my sister on our front lawn. However, I ignored the message and careened into the pampas grass while trying to retrieve a soccer ball, piercing my knee with one of the plant's wooden stalks. I learned then that the "be careful" and "edgy" messages were important. They are subtle signals that my inner contacts send to my physical body system when I am approaching danger. When heeded, these subtle messages have literally saved me from car wrecks, household accidents and spiritual experiences for which I was not prepared. When ignored, I have usually paid a price. Once you learn to distinguish and decode the signals offered to you by your physical body system, you are better equipped to react to the symptoms of spiritual disturbance before they root too deeply. When we follow the guidance offered through the subtle signals of our physical body system in reaction to any particular spiritual working or encounter, we will usually make the right decision. Remember, it is always better to play it safe than to extend ourselves beyond our spiritual capacity, so when in doubt step back.

To assist us avoid the perils of spiritually deep waters in PCA, we rely considerably on what we call the *AS AS Agreement*, which consists of a set of parameters by which all persons working with us must abide without exception. The acronym *AS AS* stands for the spiritual principle "As above, so below...As within, so without" In our practice, it reminds us that what we experience as an individual will influence the group and what occurs within the group will, in turn, influence the individual. Specifically, if the individual strays out of their depth, the group will feel the impact and vice versa. In addition to referencing the "As above, so below" axiom, *AS AS* also represents the first letter of each word of our collective agreement (see below). The *AS AS Agreement* binds us to each other as brothers and sisters engaged in the pursuit of ceremonial arts, spiritual growth and personal transformation. It also binds us to being fully awake within our spiritual and magical practices so we learn when we need help and how to seek it. Three of the *AS AS* principles simply require a person to communicate and pre-commit to a "yes" response when help is offered, the fourth requires each person to cultivate a relationship with their physical body system so that warning signs are learned, detected and heeded. Whether you work within an intimate group, a large community or solitarily, a conscious covenant of personal responsibility and accountability can go a long way toward ensuring your well being. The following four principles are the basis for our *AS AS Agreement*.

If you are working in a peer group or on your own you would modify the third principle accordingly.

The AS AS Agreement

Active Fortification – I will learn the language of my own physical body system. In addition, I will actively and consciously develop and maintain a fortification practice for my physical body system.

Self-Awareness – I will learn to recognize my own individual warning signs that signal a shift in the balance, energy and harmony of my physical body system.

Agree to Communicate – If/when I experience any of the warning signs of personal, spiritual imbalance; I will communicate this to my primary facilitators promptly and directly.

Support to Shift – If/when any warning signs are noted and communicated, I agree to actively engage in and maintain a practice that promotes and supports my own healing and the reestablishment of my physical body system's balance.

> *A chain is no stronger than its weakest link, and if one of the team cannot handle the forces, everybody is going to suffer.* [39]
> – Dion Fortune

Sometimes in an intense ritual one person will experience a ceremonial crisis that no one else experiences. This situation can create quite a ripple in the field. When this phenomenon occurs, it is likely due to one of the following reasons: 1) the individual is ill, overtired or in some other way not aware of their current state of well being, thus the working was too much for them at this particular time or 2) the individual is spiritually under-prepared for the magnitude of the particular working. Erroneously we may think that our state of being and readiness only impacts us in a group ritual and if we simply stay quiet and appear focused, we can disguise any internal blips or problems that arise during the working. Rarely is this the case. When, for whatever reason, a person in a ritual group is not able to hold and/or mediate the

---

[39] Fortune, Dion. *Psychic Self-Defense*, Weiser Books, Boston, MA/York Beach, ME, 2001, p. 92.

spiritual energies associated with their place or purpose, the ritual working and the people involved can become compromised. I have personally experienced this situation many times over the years. A person is negatively affected by a ritual; he or she blames the ritual, the group or the presiding Priest or Priestess for their bad experience. The propensity to blame another is understandable under the circumstances, yet rarely does this shoe truly fit. Normally persons such as this have not cultivated their ability to know when a magical working or ritual is within or beyond their personal scope. Lacking the ability to know when they are out of their depth, they proceed when they should not. Because their experience is unusually harsh, they look externally for the source of their discomfort. When we hear phrases like "a chain is no stronger than its weakest link" it may seem like nothing more than a cruel reiteration of proverbial Darwinism. However, if we move beyond social commentary and into the realms of physical science, we will understand the practical basis for this wisdom.

We all know that the rubber material that composes our car tires is subjected to increasing pressure when the tire is inflated. This pressure is caused by greater and greater quantities of air entering a confined space. If the tire is thinner or weaker anywhere along its form, the pressure will try to escape by bulging and eventually bursting through the thin or weak spot. Ritual workings are dynamically quite similar. When we cast a circle and call forth the unseen worlds, we are inviting increased spiritual energy into the contained field or space. If one person is unprepared or unable to meet the field of working generated by the ritual, he or she will feel the pressure in a real and compelling manner because they are, in essence, the weak spot in the containment. When we suffer inside a ritual circle, it never happens in the isolation or secrecy we think (or hope) it will. What we endure in group ritual workings, the group and ritual will also endure in some way. Thus, it is important to our own health and the health of our brothers and sisters that we know and respect our personal limitations. If you feel you could, for whatever reason, be the weak link on a particular occasion, it may be best for you and those with whom you are engaged to step back from the ritual or working.

I would like to make one final observation in this section with regard to the weakest link analogy. You may recall that earlier on, I mentioned the duress that the physical body can, and often does, endure when working outside the confines of the physical world to which it is most accustomed. In that context, acute physical symptoms such as fatigue or illness were highlighted. However, it should be mentioned that as a result of increased spiritual work, we may also develop a chronic place of structural weakness within our physical body system. Physical symptoms such as neck pain, back pain, metabolic changes, indigestion and vertigo are but a few examples of the kind of chronic ailments some spiritual practitioners experience as time goes on. In some cases, these places hold the memory of prior physical trauma or ailment which creates their vulnerability. In other cases, there is no prior trauma or ailment associated with these locations. Regardless of derivation, these physical places within us act as the escape valve for the spiritual expansion of the physical body that occurs when we engage in otherworldly practices. They are what I call our physical or spiritual "Achilles heel." When we overdo it spiritually, these already vulnerable places act like the weak spot in the tire by expressing themselves acutely to let us know we've done too much. As men and women of spirit seeking to honor the physical temple, we must attend to our spiritual Achilles heel. Some people develop a system for buffering these places inside them by doing preparatory work with that aspect of the body prior to engaging in spiritual or magical working. Some have learned they must stay out of particular fields of working altogether. Still others know how to recognize the post-spiritual working warning signs and can thwart the trouble with immediate aftercare. Don't be discouraged if you too have noticed a reoccurring physical phenomenon in response to your increased personal spiritual practices. I and many of my colleagues have our share of these troubles. Above all, we must remember these aspects of our bodies are our teachers; they keep us mindful of the physical temple and how to remain engaged in our spiritual work while attuned to our human physicality. Encouragingly, these troublesome physical aspects can and usually do improve over the course of our spiritual and magical practices. We may experience a weak spot in our physical body for years and years and then suddenly the trouble lifts due to the benefit of continued spiritual work. What is important with regard to these places is that we tend them lovingly and carefully and do not stupidly push past them such that further and deeper injury or ailment manifests.

Condition Four

"We May Fall Victim To Certain Pathological Conditions Which Rend The Veil"

In this final point, Fortune refers to ways in which the veils that separate adjacent worlds become torn or fractured by a particularly unhealthy condition or situation as opposed to being intentionally lifted through spiritual and magical workings. Conditions of rending and ripping are very important to understand for they function in a vastly different manner to the conditions of intentional spiritual engagement. As was stated previously, when we are young in our spiritual and magical work we often think that the unseen worlds are perfectly harmonious and only the physical world is marred by disease, illness and environmental stress. However, as we progress in our spiritual training and experience we realize that disease, illness and environmental stress exists in the unseen worlds as well. In mass, these conditions are referred to as otherworldly pathologies. They generally occur in two basic forms: lingering discarnate human forms and locational disturbances in the natural world. Because understanding otherworldly pathologies is foundational to a spiritual discernment practice, I will spend considerable time discussing their formation.

Death and the Pathologies of the Discarnate

Most people understand death as that which occurs when the vital organs of the physical body cease to function. However, this is only the beginning of the death process. To understand the meaning behind this statement it is important to obtain a basic understanding of the normal progression of death. Dion Fortune's *Book of the Dead*[40] offers an excellent and very readable account of this process; what follows is a brief summary.

After the physical body ceases to function, the soul and etheric double of the deceased become slowly demagnetized so that the soul may leave this life and journey forward through the other layers and processes of the death cycle. The complete demagnetization of the soul and etheric double of the physical body can take up to three days. This is why it is so important for the physical body to be handled carefully during the initial

---

[40]Fortune, Dion. *Dion Fortune's Book of the Dead*, Weiser Press, York Beach ME, 1995.

post-death phase as any jarring or rough handling can thwart the separation process.

Deaths caused by traumatic and unnatural means circumvent the organized progression within which a complete and unhindered death occurs. When death is sudden, traumatic or caused by a debilitating disease that disturbs a person's conscious ability to surrender to the process of life's release, disorientation can result. This disorientation can encourage the person to cling to their earthly life and the etheric double from which they ought to separate. Disallowed the graceful separation within the natural death process, the consciousness of the person becomes fractured. This fracturing causes some aspects of the self to be left behind. If, when this occurs, the soul retains its magnetic hold upon the etheric double for a considerable amount of time that which is left behind will begin to take on the form and function of a progressively pathological entity. In this manner, pathologically discarnate beings become part of the field of negative/retarding spiritual beings and energies spoken of thus far.

Victims of violent crimes, war and other tragic circumstances can easily fall prey to the spiritual and physical fracturing just described. A friend of mine, also a seer, lived two blocks from the old gang quarter in downtown Chicago. She was often visited by discarnate young men who had fallen victim to sudden gang violence. These youths either did not realize they were dead or due to its suddenness and their young age, resisted the notion in a state of panic and fear. As a result their spirits roamed the area around which they died and would, on occasion, waft through her apartment. She did her best to assist them in finding their way through and out of this life completely; however, many were overly attached to the emotional circumstances of their untimely death and could only function within the field of vengeance. Spiritually immature humans traumatized by a premature death such as this often remain connected to the earthly realms by virtue of their desire for revenge and restitution. Beings attached to their earthly life in this manner often believe they are as solid a physical form as they when they were alive. Due to this attachment, they stay rooted somewhat to their etheric double and the physical realms within which they lived and died, often living on in the perpetual state of fear, anger or confusion that accompanied their death. In this way, discarnate beings remain active upon the subtle planes until some physical or metaphysical action shifts their course.

We have discussed the afterlife perils that confront those who experience a shocking or sudden death; however persons dying normally may also be challenged during death thus becoming re-attracted to their physical body and earthly life. Within the Western Esoteric Tradition (and other traditions as well) it is understood that life after death consists of a significant period of personal review and reconciliation that is guided by otherworldly assistants. This process takes several earthly years to complete. As spiritual practitioners, it is important that we understand the life review process that the departed becomes engaged in after death and do not inadvertently circumvent its progress through our spiritual and magical work.

Along these lines it is important to understand that there are helpful ways of communicating with the dead and unhelpful ways. If, as a man or woman of spirit, we wish to lovingly assist the dead with their transition, we may choose to be in touch with them. When we do so, we should focus our efforts on the means of communication that encourage the dead to move through their process.

During the initial post-death phase it can be helpful to speak words of encouragement to the departed. Provided we retain our clear understanding of their need to progress onward, encouraging prayer and recitation can also be very comforting to those navigating the death process. In some cultures the living actually take turns reading heartening stories or poetry aloud to the dead in support of their afterlife journey. If you sense a deceased person close to you is having a hard time moving on, reading aloud the steps of the death process contained in Dion Fortune's *Book of the Dead* and other similar texts can assist. In all cases, it is important that those of us left behind by the death of a loved one do our best to ensure the dead that we will be fine and bear no ill will towards them. If you know a deceased person has unfinished business with you, it can be helpful to relieve them of their concern and attachment by assuring them that you forgive them and will remember them for their best and forget the rest. If we engage in emotionally needy or aggressive communications with the dead, we may inadvertently encourage the re-attraction of the departed one's soul to its etheric double. For the dead ready to journey onward, nothing is worse than being repeatedly called backwards to console, engage with or provide guidance to the living.

In situations where the departed had little or no spiritual knowledge or faith-based practice in life, a clinging to the familiarity of the physical world can occur. As noted previously, when the dead do not move on, they initially retain many of their human characteristics. However, as time progresses, the human characteristics fade, fragmentation occurs and parasitic characteristics begin to materialize. The goal is of course to assist the departed to move away from their attachments to the physical world as quickly and cleanly as possible. As spiritual practitioners, it is important to understand beings unfamiliar with the spiritual teachings of the afterlife can easily become lost when confronted by this transition. To these persons, the unseen world to which they've transitioned is a very unfamiliar place. The physical world is not as solid as it once was, but at least it is familiar; thus they cling to what they know. As men and women of spirit, our goal is to turn the attention of the departed away from the physical world and toward the otherworldly hosts that await them. As mentioned a moment ago, there are beings on the other side that specialize in assisting the souls of the dead through their complete transition. We must allow these beings to do their work. This allowing means we do not engage in silly rituals that aggravate or frighten the dead. Take a moment to remember a time when you got lost traveling about and had no idea how to get from where you were to where you wanted to go. If in that moment of confusion, concern and anxiety, an aggressive and righteous passer by accosted you for being lost what would that have done to your state? We must remember over and over again, that even though the seen and unseen worlds are structurally different, nearly all the foundational principles of the seen world apply to the unseen world. Spiritual activities such as random exorcisms, demanding the dead to "move on", energetic clearings and the like usually only make the situation worse. If instead we call to the most exalted Divine with whom we work, while tenderly redirecting the attentions of the departed to the presence of compassionate spiritual beings that preside over these transitions, most of the lost and confused dead will find their way home.

It is true that some human beings specialize in releasing the lost and confused departed between the post-death and prepathological phases of existence. However, in all cases, they work within a partnership of specialized spiritual allies. The spiritual work of liberation should not be attempted by well meaning yet uneducated men and women of spirit. In my personal experience and in speaking with others who have also assisted in this manner, threshold crossing work is initiated by our Higher Self in conjunction with appropriate inner contacts. In other words, we don't choose this work, it chooses us. I did not wake up one day in my cheery, occultist identity thinking to myself "I believe I will valiantly dedicate the fruits of my abilities to assisting the dead in their otherworldly transitions." Instead, I experienced a spiritual dream-based visitation that offered this work as an option that I might, over time and with otherworldly education, learn to perform. This dream-based visitation occurred five years ago. Since then, I have only been called upon to assist with the failed crossing of one woman and two men who became lost during the death process. I will briefly recount the story of the woman to illustrate the nature of this work to those who feel they may also have been called into this service.

A few years ago I learned of the wrongful death of a woman who was close to some of our PCA members. Several months later, one of her friends came to me concerned for the spiritual well being of this woman who she felt near her when she was engaged in ceremonial work. Feeling the woman was attracted to the spiritual work of her friends, she asked me if I could help her complete the death transition. I told her I may be able to help, but that we should just wait to see what the spiritual forces presiding over her death dictated and what opportunities arose. I made no other gestures or plans to assist this woman; from here. Two weeks after this conversation, the murdered woman appeared in my dreams. She was seated cross-legged and firm within the injustice of her death. In the dream, I approached her body offering a point of human contact and comfort. I was then guided to help release her soul's attachment through a series of specific gestures and spoken words. Once this was complete, I was guided to symbolically bury the frame of her physical form and the tragedy of its death. In this work, there was no gallant waving of crystal wands or making of chants ignorant of the spiritual beings that are better suited to assist. I simply offered a comforting human form that could receive and execute the spiritual guidance and power of those who knew how to attend to this wronged and grieving woman before her fragmentation progressed any further.

As was mentioned previously, not all fragmented beings are a function of unpremeditated or confused deaths. Sometimes living beings fragment by virtue of an inability or unwillingness to release their attachment to a person, place or thing. When I was a child I lived in a part of Kansas that had a very strong Native American ancestral presence. In our town, it was well known that one particular Native American woman named Sophie haunted the college dormitory that bore her name; in essence, the building itself and its commemorative significance held her there in some way. Our dear friends who were caretakers of this dormitory often told tales of Sophie's disturbed wanderings about the place. Not until the building was torn down and the native stones of its construction scattered was Sophie able to release her attachment and move on. In another respect, the love we have for a place in life can keep us in its attendance after death. In the book *The Gate of Remembrance*[41] Frederick Bligh Bond relays the story of the otherworldly contact he fostered between himself, his working partner and the deceased monks of Glastonbury Abbey, in 1907. Assisted by the technique known as automatic writing, the monks of Glastonbury Abbey assisted Bond and his partner in excavating some of the lost structures within the Abbey grounds. In this case, love of the Abbey and its sacred work created a bond between these deceased holy men and the place they served.

Unhealthy Natural Systems

Natural systems can also become diseased and manifest pathological life forms. Unhealthy patterns in nature often exist where the inherent cycles of cleansing and purification have become disturbed or negatively imprinted. In the case of a disturbance, a natural system's cleansing mechanisms may be blocked or altered by human activity. When humans build too many homes on a wetland region blocking the life cycle of the marsh or strip mine gold from the hills and allow the tailings to flow into nearby water sources, we disturb the natural cleansing and purification cycle. Likewise, when we fight bloody battles upon

---

[41] Bond, Frederick Bligh. *The Gate of Remembrance, Collector's Library of the Unknown*, Time-Life Books, Alexandria VA; originally published by B.H. Blackwell, Broad Street, Oxford UK, 1918.

the land or suicide bomb innocent people in our cities, we create an imprint on the natural environment there. Thought-forms that motivate one human being to strike another dead possess an undeniable power in and of themselves. That which is created during violent acts of war and death lingers. When situations of mass action such as battles of war or terrorist activities occur, the sheer force of the condensed anger, hatred or fear manifested in these actions leaves an imprint upon a place. Over time violent and hate-based thought-forms create their own manifestations, separate from the human consciousness involved in their initial creation[42].

To those attuned to the currents and frequencies of the natural world, it is usually subtly obvious when a place is disturbed or imprinted. Such places tend to emit a particular vibration or sensation detectable to our physical body system and our sacred imagination. In the mid 1990s, I learned that in many cases, the degree of disturbance in a natural setting is scientifically measurable as well. One fall evening in 1997, I attended a lecture offered by a scientist who concluded several years traveling in the United States taking magnetic readings at spiritual sites such as the prayerfully inscribed petroglyphs of the Southwest and the violently impressed witch hunting sites in the Northeast. In the many positively and negatively imprinted sites he tested, the magnetic readings he measured in these sites showed a higher frequency than sites sites void of such well known human imprints. The data he put forth that night was remarkable and quite convincing. In concluding his lecture, he left the audience with two questions. Is it the site that naturally possesses the increased frequency thus drawing the humans to it? Or is it the human activity that occurred there responsible for creating the change in the magnetic atmosphere of the place? As a woman of spirit trained in the mechanics of the astral realm and humanity's ability to imprint it, I default to the later explanation. But in either case, it is interesting to realize that the hard sciences are increasingly verifying the intuitive knowledge and understanding of the esoteric community.

As was mentioned earlier, spiritual practitioners are often drawn to the places and situations where we may help restore

---

[42]Fortune, Dion. *Dion Fortune's Book of the Dead*, Weiser Press, York Beach ME, 1995.

harmony and balance. In the case of a natural setting, the damage usually begins with unhealthy physical changes perpetuated by ignorant human activities that, over time, lead to the formation of an unhealthy natural environment. Where clearly visible environmental degradation is the obvious cause of a natural setting's imbalance, as in the case of polluted lands, dumping of unwanted materials or blocked waterways, physical remediation is beginning to take place. Over the course of the past few decades, several governmental agencies have started to engage in the work of environmental remediation from a purely physical understanding of the problems we've created in the Earth's natural systems. We have not yet become sophisticated enough to create agencies that specialize in the remediation of the energetic human imprints that have fostered pathological conditions upon the land. This work remains the responsibility of the men and women of spirit who spend time and energy learning how to assist in these matters. When degrading imprints such as those left by pollution, conflict and war are the cause of distress in a natural system, human remediation may also be needed. In other cases, if we simply back away and leave the environment alone, it will restore itself. When we can and should assist in a natural system's energetic remediation, the work required of us is of course subtle and much less quantifiable in conventional terms. For this reason, it is important to develop our capacity to humbly listen to the distresses and needs of the setting in question before engaging in any way. The spiritual beings that preside over these places are in charge and we are simply human agents offering a uniquely different form of benevolent contact (as opposed to that which degraded the lands) in order to restore the balance between the beings of the seen and unseen worlds. In these situations, Frank MacEowen's *The Cycle* meditation offered in the Methods and Applications section of this book is highly recommended as a starting point.

In many cases of natural system pathologies, both the physical and the energetic environment need our attention. I will offer an example from my work where a combination of both physical and metaphysical work was needed to reestablish the harmony of a natural setting. One summer some friends and I visited a wilderness area a few hundred miles from Boulder. The site was tended by a community of people who lived and worked on the land. Our stay that summer coincided with bear hunting season; had we known, we would have likely picked another time to visit. One evening near the end of our stay, we witnessed the death of one of the land's yearling bear cubs perpetuated by a group of local hunters. Not only did we witness this bear's death, we were standing in the direct pathway through which the life force and energy of the bear was powerfully released. Understanding the implications of this, we prepared our sleeping quarters to the best of our ability. At the time, we did not realize that the spiritual work that staves off nighttime contact with wandering human spirits does little to ward off contact with wandering primal spirits. During the night that followed, I experienced one of the most challenging spiritual practicums of my life. Just after midnight, I became engrossed in three very intense and physically possessive otherworld transmissions; for lack of a better term I will call them dreams. During the first dream, I was guided into a library, down a corridor and through a swinging door. Dream images such as these usually alert us to the fact that we are entering into the adjacent worlds; they give us the option to continue or turn back. As it was, I chose to cross the threshold into an adjacent world that night. In the second dream, the door to my sleeping quarters crashed open. A spirit man stood at the threshold of the room and did not enter. The dead bear's spirit charged into the room and leapt on top of my bed and my body; its breathing was heavy and intense. The aggressive and instinctually-driven spirit of the bear was inches away from my face; I was truly afraid of its potential to attack. In the third dream, the bear and the man engaged my personal faculties. I was walking in the body of the man, but conversing with a growling, bear like voice. This was terrifying and required an enormous amount of my vital energy to sustain. The grace of this third dream was the message the man and bear endeavored to relay to me. In their partnership, the man and the bear showed me how upset they were with increased structural building and human activities taking place on this wilderness land and I knew I was to convey their message to the community that tended it. When the third dream's hold was released, I awoke gasping for air and in need of physical assistance from my roommate to revive. Later that morning while conveying the night's activities to the head of the community, as I felt I was to do, I was informed that a man who owned and tended the land was murdered there several years earlier when his joint owner wanted to sell and he did not. This man died in reverence to the land he loved. The description of the spirit man I offered the caretakers matched the description of the man they knew. What I realized during this very intense and powerful experience is that the spirit of the bear and the spirit of the man had come together in the adjacent world for a particular purpose, a common connection and a desire to shift the state of affairs where they had lived. The caretakers of the land heeded the messages and performed a loving remembrance and gratitude ceremony for the bear and the man. They agreed to reexamine their plans to build new structures on the land which would draw more people into its wilderness. I walked away from this experience thoroughly exhausted and much, much wiser as to the nature of these matters.

When we visit the places where unhealthy energies exist we will tend to experience one of two effects. Out of a need for vital energy, the spirits and energies of the place may draw us in just like the parasitic beings we described earlier. In these scenarios we will become drained, dizzy, nauseous or devitalized in some manner just as we would when encountering a discarnate being. Secondly, out of a total distrust of and disgust for humanity, the land-based spiritual beings who dwell there may push us away by relaying subtle and not-so-subtle messages. Many of us have heard of or experienced feelings of unwelcome expressed by beings of the unseen worlds that inhabit a particular place and want nothing to do with humankind. In one manner these beings are simply frayed and fragmented from the traumas inflicted into their dwellings by the senseless acts of humanity. Seeking solace, they view our presence as a threat to their well being. In another manner, these place-based beings may simply be protective of the land, waters, plants and animals they tend.

I tend a particular sacred site on the land near our temple; a year or so after beginning this work I became aware of a Native American ancestor whose spirit dwells near the site. This man watched my tending regime and the actions of the spiritual circles that gathered there as if interested; however, he never ventured close or participated. One day I went to the site and asked the man why he stayed so far back in the trees during our ritual workings. Did he disapprove of our presence here? In response, I felt both a sense of extended curiosity and frustration with the white humans that had come and gone since his life ended on this land. I felt he would continue to watch us from his distance for he expected we would be no different than the others. I still journey to this site and oftentimes feel him watching from between the trees. Given the strength of his convictions, I doubt his manner will change in my lifetime.

To summarize, discarnate beings may become lost and confused by their death and thus re-attach themselves to their human life in an increasingly pathological manner. Natural systems impacted in some way by unhealthy human or spiritual activities can also develop pathological characteristics. As mentioned previously, in these situations the discontented spiritual beings and energies often need assistance to free themselves and move onward. In other cases, even if assisted, some pathological beings and energies have no interest in moving on. Human and nature-based pathologies tend to function in a parasitic manner, by drawing upon on other life forces. Void of a Divinely created source of vital energy, these beings and energies draw upon the vital energy of humans, plants and animals to maintain their existence. Their need for vital energy is the primary means by which their presence distresses us. Let us now move on to a discussion of these distresses, their effects and what we can do about them.

The Distresses and Impacts of Otherworldly Pathologies Upon the Physical Body System

Though the two forms of parasitic spiritual beings and energies discussed in this section have distinct manifestations, the effect they have upon our physical body system is quite similar. For the most part, negative/retarding spiritual beings and energies work through the mechanisms of thought-form and thought-force. In a prior section, the concept of a though-form was discussed at length; however the term thought-force is new to our discourse. Thought-force is a creation of pure consciousness that is not situated within any geographical position. It connects itself to a particular subtle resonance in an unseen world and thus manifests wherever that resonance is called into consciousness or form. One example of a negative/retarding thought-force is degrading and violent lyrics encased within some rap or heavy metal music. When played, sung or otherwise recreated, the malicious thought-force manifests instantly in the person, space or place. As you will recall, thought-form is quite different. It has position in space via its attachment, but it does not occupy physical space, but adjuncts the physical space energetically. Once created a thought-form can and will remain within the magnetic field of the place or object until it dissipates or gathers enough power and focus to become autonomous. If we understand that thought-forms and thought-forces are the primary means of influence utilized by negative/retarding spiritual beings and energies, we can piece together their effect.[43] By and large this effect relies upon the same systematization inside our consciousness as it does in the subtle planes. In the following excerpt, Dion Fortune aptly describes the route of entry and physical/psychic effect of parasitic beings and unhealthy natural energies.

> *Until the aura is pierced there can be no entrance to the soul, and the aura is always pierced from within by the response of fear or desire going out toward the attacking entity. If we can inhibit that instinctive emotional reaction, the edge of the aura will remain impenetrable and will be as sure a defense against psychic invasion as the healthy and unbroken skin is a defense against bacterial infection*[44] – Dion Fortune

As Dion Fortune instructs, our susceptibility to the effects of any particular malevolent thought-form or thought-force is a function of our personal affinity for the circumstance it projects onto us. Typically these affinities are a function of our own unhealed fears, prior wounds, ancestral ties or cellular memories. In my experience, some sophisticated parasitic beings posses an ability to scan human beings to determine the most effective means of entrapment. Because this is so, it behooves us to know and heal our vulnerable, inner landscapes so we are less susceptible to the influences of unhealthy discarnate beings and energies.

If we are unfortunate enough to find ourselves entrapped by a parasitic being or energy, we must first and foremost endeavor to break the connection. If we can literally change our location, we should by all means do so as this is the most direct means of breaking the connection. Our next objective is to arrest any distressing or seductive emotional responses this being or energy has aroused within us. Shifting our proximity to the

---

[43] Fortune, Dion. *Psychic Self-Defense*, Weiser Books, Boston, MA/York Beach ME, 2001.

[44] Ibid. pp 16-17.

unhealthy beings and energies and then shifting the reactions of our consciousness are the two important steps which close the portals to their entry. As an example, let us say you're traveling about staying in historic bed and breakfasts along the eastern seaboard. On the first night in historic inn, you've found yourself enticed into an unhealthy sexual or survival dreamscape. Because you are now aware of this favorite route of the pathological beings and energies you are more alert to this occurrence. Thus in the dream, some part of your consciousness is able to become awake or lucid. You remember that first you must break the psychic connection or avert the action of the unhealthy dreamscape. Often this is done by confronting a character within the dream that appears to be its perpetuator. Once, while initially engaged in a survival dream, I yelled "Stop!" at the top of my lungs while still inside the dream. At that moment, the whole scene ceased its motion; the lead actor in the dream looked at me in a startled manner and left the frame thus ending the unhealthy dreamscape. Once this perpetuator is confronted, you will usually notice holes in the tapestry the parasitic beings or energies are working to weave. These holes are your means to unravel the attachment and release the parasitic being's grip on your physical body system. Once the connection is broken, you must shift your consciousness out of the state into which the dream enticed you. As long as the feelings of fear, anxiety or arousal are lingering inside you, you will continue to be affected by the presence and influence of the unhealthy beings or energies. This can involve actually getting up, out of bed and taking a shower or a bath immediately. Often I will use a combination of salt and olive oil or salt and honey as these substances help to reconfigure and realign the subtle energies of the physical body system impacted by an unhealthy interaction. From here you may need to change your sleeping location within the inn as these beings usually don't function well in change. This can be achieved by moving you pillow to the foot of the bed or sleeping on the couch. Finally, it will most undoubtedly require you to call upon the benevolent Higher Forces with whom you work for support through the remainder of the night. In the morning you can decide whether to stay another night in the inn or move onward.

Most parasitic beings rely on the under-education of the normal human being who does not know the dynamics of the unseen worlds. Parasitic beings and energies do not normally choose to work hard. When they stumble upon a person who is wise to their means of entrapment and challenges them, they will usually disengage and move on to a more unwitting victim. By virtue of our own knowledge, vigilance and learned ability to disengage, we can do a lot to arrest parasitic invasions. It should also be known that on some occasions the sophistication of the beings encountered is such that our mere knowledge of their ways and challenges will do little to discourage their actions. These advanced beings have cultivated a strong field of form and force around them, making them much more difficult to dissuade. In these circumstances we will need to actively enlist the help of our spiritual allies in the unseen worlds. In the Methods and Applications section of this book, the importance of building bridges between ourselves and our allies in the unseen worlds will be emphasized. I will also discuss the virtue of knowing and declaring ourselves spiritually in such a way that helpful beings are drawn to us and malevolent beings dispelled. As a precursor to these later discussions, in this section our attentions have been focused on understanding the conditions of cause. If we do not understand how the negative/retarding energies and beings of adjacent worlds function, our practical actions are weakly based.

I've discussed the manner in which pathological beings and energies impact us during our sleep, what can we expect when we encounter them during the awakened parts of our day? In these circumstances, our physical body system becomes depleted by a parasitic draw of our vital energy in much the same manner but without the interplay of story and drama that meet us in our sleep. In waking circumstances we can experience many different symptoms of spiritual disturbance including, but not limited to, unpleasant smells, stagnation of air, headaches, emotional aggravation, nausea or sudden exhaustion. Mired within the psychic cloud that these beings work to create, we may also stubbornly resist leaving the place or circumstance, which allows the being to continue drawing vital energy from our physical body system. When in our waking life, we find ourselves inexplicably unnerved, exhausted, irritated or ill in a physical environment, as men and women of spirit, we must consider the possibility of a locational disturbance. One reliable test of this potential is to leave the environment and notice any differences. Once while laboring my way through dinner in an unhealthy restaurant, I suddenly realized just how drained and almost sick I'd become. When I simply walked outside, moment by moment everything began to shift, and my sense of well being returned.

Normally, parasitic beings are able to pierce our consciousness through one of two ways: first by tapping into our self-preservation instincts and second by tapping into our sexual instincts.[45] Both of these instincts are deeply seated within the human psyche and are thus natural hooks for discarnate beings to locate and exploit. When awake, this can manifest in a stubbornness to stay in a place that we know is devitalizing us or to become overly sentimentalize or naively attached to the particular environment or situation. When asleep and thus divorced from the state of acuity we possess when we are awake, an invasion of the dreaming nature is easier for the imposing entity to muster.

As offered in the historic inn example just mentioned, when we find ourselves in a location where discarnate entities linger, we may repeatedly experience dreams of seduction or endurance for our own or another's survival. In these instances, the enticing dreams keep us wrapped in sleep for a much longer period than our body normally requires. Unable to retain the vital energy that normally accumulates in the sleeping hours, our physical body does not experience the normal build to waking. We stay asleep longer due to a consistent drain of vital energy and when we finally do awaken, we are unusually fatigued. This is not to say that all sexual and seductive or survival dreams are the work of parasitic discarnate beings. Often these dreams are simply the means by which our conscious and subconscious mind integrates the previous day or alerts us to the condition of our own psychological or physical well being. However, if you find that these dreams repeat and repeat for no discernable personal reason, it would behoove you to consider the potential of a parasitic assault. Whether through asleep or awaking, the objective of a pathological being or energy is to keep our physical body system entangled for as long as possible so it may continue to extract the vital energy it needs to exist in its "in-between" form.

In this Foundations and Definitions section of the book, I have relayed information pertinent to the nature of negative/retarding spiritual beings and energies via four pivotal questions.

---

[45]Fortune, Dion. *Psychic Self Defense*, Weiser Books, Boston, MA/York Beach, ME, 2001. pp 15.

I will repeat them again for reference as we momentarily take stock of the territory we've covered. Referencing the principles of impact and all of the information that followed, you should now be confident in your ability to answer each of these four questions. Before moving on to Methods and Applications section of this book, I would recommend you take a moment to test yourself. Without looking at the prior pages, write the answers to each question in your journal. When you have done this to the best of your ability, refer to the prior pages to capture any details you missed. With this foundation in place, we are now ready to develop our own practice of spiritual discernment.

1.   How specifically do the energies and/or beings of adjacent worlds impact us and by what means can they invade our physical body system?

2.   How is it that one person engaged in a ritual working can be inordinately affected by a particular unseen force while others remain comparatively unaffected? What determines our susceptibility to the influences of the unseen worlds?

3.   If we are negatively affected by a particular otherworldly force, how do we know when it is safe to reengage in our spiritual and magical work?

4.   What is our best defense against the negative and invasive forces of adjacent worlds?

Methods and Applications

If we are not willing to clear evils from our own self-circles we have no right to complain of them elsewhere, nor any power to prevent them there either. The keys of exorcising our entire earth lie with each individual living therein...(if they would do their own work to banish personal evils) they would make a most positive contribution towards decreasing its influence elsewhere. [46] – W.G. Gray

Making It Real

For those of us truly interested in furthering our spiritual and magical work, a commitment to developing and maintaining a personal practice of spiritual discernment is paramount. When we enlist ourselves into the co-creative rites of adjacent worlds, a normal life structured around a balance of work, rest, personal, family and community well being is no longer sufficient. There is nothing wrong with this particular scope or focus; for many it provides the foundation for an admirable life. However, if you wish to include the well being of the relationship between the seen and unseen worlds among your occupations, your personal habits and patterns must be supplemented to reflect this choice.

In PCA we use the phrase "make it real" quite often. This phrase reminds us that the spiritual aspects of our lives must be aligned with the other aspects of our lives in real and concrete ways. Many can "talk the talk" easily enough, but unless we can "walk the walk", we are not truly making our spiritual

---

[46] Gray, William G. *Exorcising the Tree of Evil*, Kima Global Publishers, Cape Town South Africa 2002, p 204.

115

work real. Thus, both the preparations for and actuation of our spiritual and magical work must manifest in ways that complement and bolster our habits, occupation, responsibilities, living situation, financial realities and the needs of our physical body system. Adding anything additional to the complex structure of our modern life can be arduous; which may be the reason that few persons migrate from "talking the talk" to "walking the walk." For those of us who do, a personal spiritual practice becomes no more or less important than any other practical matter of our lives, for it is though this practice that we maintain balance and wellness throughout the whole of it all.

Additionally, if you choose to deepen and expand your spiritual and magical work, you will notice that your otherworldly awareness changes and grows. Even small amounts of spiritual and magical work will open doors and windows to new subtle experiences. No shift in otherworldly awareness occurs in only one direction; when spiritually induced changes in our awareness manifest, we are broadened in a spectrum-like manner. As our healing and harmonizing meditations and magical workings increase in frequency and effectiveness, our awareness of and susceptibility to the negative/retarding spiritual beings and energies will also increase. We must take stock in this natural duality of expanding spiritual capacity and prepare ourselves for its effects.

If you believe you can familiarize yourself with and basically follow the guidance that forms the basis of a spiritual discernment practice and be met with success, you are mistaken. To be effective, this particular spiritual occupation requires a commitment to earnest application and discipline. This is not meant to sound overly terse. Think of it this way: it is hard enough for us to apply ourselves successfully to the aspects of our lives that we can objectively witness and measure. When we expand ourselves in such a way that we include working with the unseen worlds, we have to realize this work does not offer the same capacity for objectivity and measurement. To most of us, the unseen worlds are not overtly visible, touchable, or in any way concretely tangible; they are subtle. This fact adds a certain challenge to our lives. For we must build (or remember and reform) a capacity within ourselves that allows us to work in conditions that are not clearly apparent, yet are very real. Because our normal ways of doing and being are not enough for us to rely upon when performing our spiritual work, we must apply ourselves to developing and maintaining extraordinary ways of doing and being. Further, we must do this in real and practicable ways that are compatible with the rest of our lives. These ways necessitate application and discipline beyond what is generally required of us in the physical world and we have to earnestly attend to that application and any changes that it demands of us.

Observing Your State of Being

As is nearly always the case, any approach to a change of habit or routine is better founded when it is built in recognition of baseline conditions. Because our baseline consciousness weighs so heavily on the course of our spiritual and magical work, in building a spiritual discernment practice we begin by observing our current mental and emotional state. In contrast to the "ready-set-go" methods sometimes recommended, I believe it is best to begin any advancement of our personal spiritual habits and patterns by first spending a set amount of time observing our current occupations. This not only includes an observation of our thoughts, deeds and emotions, it also includes an assessment of our personal motivations for thinking, feeling and willing[47]. With these data in hand, we can more compassionately and clearly alter our lives to incorporate the kinds of changes we believe will provide greater continuity between our mundane and spiritual pursuits.

To begin assessing your baseline condition of consciousness, set aside a particular amount of time that you feel will provide enough of an occasion for you to witness yourself objectively. I would recommend spending at least a month observing your baseline patterning in contemplation of the questions put forth below. Remember, as with any solemn pursuit, there are no shortcuts. You must spend the time you intuit you need to obtain a clear picture of your starting place; anything less will provide inadequate baseline information and could in fact taint the effectiveness of any practical methods you employ afterward. If you are going to practice the spiritual and magical arts, I implore you to do so offering your utmost to each and every task; again, anything less will produce little to no actual benefit and could result in harm. During this time period of personal as-

---

[47] The phrase, "thinking, feeling, willing" refers to the work of Rudolph Steiner, who coined this phrase as a reflection of the sacred actions unique to the human being. Thinking, feeling and willing are all acts that shape and transform our inner world or consciousness.

sessment, record all questions and observations in the journal you've acquired for this work.

Below are the questions to focus upon during your observation period. Questions one through six should be asked several times within your observation period; if you choose a daily assessment for a period of two weeks, then you would answer each of these questions fresh each day. If you are choosing a weekly assessment for a period of four to eight weeks, then you would perhaps answer these questions every Sunday, taking stock of the prior week's occupations. The timeframe put forth within these questions (referenced as "today or this week") is intended to encompass these possibilities. The objective is to repeat these questions several times during the observation period as multiple answers accommodate the natural ebbs and flows of your daily life and thus reflect a more thorough and accurate baseline inquiry. Questions seven through ten only need to be considered once and should thus be answered toward the end of your observation period. To clarify what is meant by the inquiry, several of the questions are followed by italicized examples of fitting responses. I recommend that you cease reading forward until you have completed your personal inquiry.

1. What matters and issues most occupied my mind (today/this week) and what do I feel motivated this baseline mental occupation?

Answer 1: *My work "to do" list occupied my mind most of my time today/this week; I feel this was motivated by the fear of getting behind.*

Answer 2: *The act of daydreaming on the pleasures of my life occupied me most today/this week; I believe this was motivated by a general state of happiness I feel growing within me now.*

2. How many hours did I spend watching movies, television or national or local news and playing computer games or surfing the web today/this week? (Be exact.)

3. In what manner did I generally think of or how did I experience other people in my life today/this week and what motivated my thoughts or experiences?

Answer 1: Most of the time I regard others with suspicion; I think this is a function of the tumultuous family life I sustained as a child.

Answer 2: I tend to regard others with compassion; I believe this is due to my personal commitment to non-judgment.

4. How much time per day do I spend in quiet contem-

plation, meditation or performing my own inner work? How, specifically, do I utilize this time?

Answer 1: *I spend 10 minutes in morning meditation each day.*

Answer 2: *I spend no time particular amount of time in a period of quiet reflection, it happens sporadically for me.*

5.   How much time per day do I spend tending my physical body in the form of eating healthy food, drinking enough water and exercising?

Answer 1: *I spend 20 minutes in morning yoga, take supplements and try to drink one quart of water daily.*

Answer 2: *I walk to and from work three days a week.*

6.   What was my general quality of sleep last night/last week? Can I detect any recognizable dream patterns during sleep during this observation period OR throughout my life in general?

Answer 1: *I sleep well and experience pleasant or restorative dreams most of the time.*

Answer 2: *I sleep restlessly and tend to have dreams about my anxieties or worries in life.*

Answer 3: *I sleep soundly and do not recall my dreams; I don't know that I have any.*

7.   What is my general orientation to the unseen worlds?

Answer 1: *In general, I do not think much about the "unseen worlds" and then suddenly I will have an experience that reminds me of their presence.*

Answer 2: *I regard the unseen worlds with a bit of suspicion.*

Answer 3: *I yearn for a deeper connection to the beings of the unseen worlds and want to cultivate this.*

8.   Describe, in some detail, the three or four most profound personal, spiritual experiences you have had. Assess what overall patterns of engagement or effects occur within each of these experiences.

9.   Walk around your home; open cupboards, file drawers, closets, look in the basement, the attic and the garage. What is the current state of the "unseen places of accumulation" in your home?

10. Finally, how long has it been since you assessed, cleansed and reconsecrated any and all ritual items or altars you have created within or around your home?

When your observation period is complete, you should have a set of statements that describe your baseline mental, social, meditative, spiritual and physical/spatial patterns on various occasions. The quality and effectiveness of your personal practice of spiritual discernment depends largely on your ability to accurately assess your baseline state. After completing the data gathering stage, take a few days to assess each of your answers. With questions one through six, try to aggregate the various answers provided into generalizations wherever possible. Focus your efforts on finding the overarching thematic pattern that best describes your common response to each of these inquiries. Once you have arrived at an aggregated assessment of questions one through six, write one to three summary statements for each question. With questions seven through ten, spend time double checking your one answer to be sure it accurately reflects what is most often true for you, even if you are not comfortable with the honest answer. From here, you will need to find time at your altar. Your purpose there is to gain any additional truth or wisdom from your inner contacts with regard to your baseline state of consciousness.

Inner Contacts Meditation

To begin the meditation that finalizes your personal observation period, find twenty minutes to meditate at your altar. Bring your body and being into stillness in preparation for meditation. Once still and ready to engage, light a candle, create your sacred sphere and call to your inner contacts. Then speak a prayer within which you request your inner contacts and the angelic beings of Truth and Wisdom to draw close to you. Speak aloud question one and your aggregated answer to this question. Now pause here and open to the inner realms, receptive to any additional information that your inner contacts or the angelic beings of Trust and Wisdom would offer you with regard to this question. When complete, make any additional notes to record the new input and proceed to question two. Continue this sequence of speaking the question, speaking your answer and opening in stillness to additional spiritual input until you have completed all ten points of inquiry. Record all additional information received into your journal and then rest for at least three days before continuing.

Once three days have passed you are ready to begin the work of creating your practice. Each aspect of this practice is referenced in the pages that follow. As you journey through the subsequent pages, be awake to and aware of the aspects of your personal observation that you know need additional attention. As you do this, be kind to yourself and remember human beings are fluid; we shift and change over time. We only become stuck if we fall asleep within our own lives and states of being. As long as we are alert to and aware of ourselves and our patterns of engagement, we can change and grow. There should be no shame or judgment assessed upon yourself as a result of this observation exercise. Instead, be encouraged by the fact that you have just engaged in the ultimate act of self love and self care which will only enhance your spiritual and magical practices.

At the point of recommencing your reading, five baseline personal patterns vital to a practice of spiritual discernment have been revealed to you. You have observed your daily mental occupation or how you routinely think. You have observed your social tendencies in both a personal and relational manner. You have assessed the amount of time you spend in reflection and repose as well as the amount of time you spend engaged in applied spiritual growth. Finally, you have assessed the relative degree of physical/spatial harmony within which you live your life. As a function of performing this personal inquiry you will very likely no longer be ignorant of these aspects of yourself. Awake and aware of your deeper personal tendencies and baseline condition of consciousness, you are better equipped to develop and incorporate a spiritual discernment practice into your daily life.

The five aspects you've just assessed join together to form *The Pentacle of Spiritual Discernment*, which serves as the foundation for our continued work. As we recognize the four sacred elements and directions that are Earth, Air, Fire and Water, we know that the pentacle is a representation of the element of Earth. The Earth element encompasses our physical foundation, health, stability and well being. In a practice of spiritual discernment, the pentacle is an apt symbol for it reminds us that though we may engage effectively with the beings and energies of otherworlds, we live on the Earth, in physical spaces and in physical bodies. While we may extend ourselves beyond its bounds, our touchstone is the physical world. Each point of the pentacle is in equal relationship to the others and all are encompassed within a circle of wholeness. These five points and the circle that encases them form the foundation of the particular spiritual discernment practice this book hopes to foster within you.

Before moving on, find time to gather a few art supplies together and create three or four copies of *The Pentacle of Spiritual Discernment* as a new point of reference in your life and surroundings. Place a copy on your altars, your car visor, by your computer, on your night table or on the bathroom mirror. Let this symbol and all it represents be a daily reminder of your commitment to maintaining personal health and well being throughout your otherworldly pursuits.

The Pentacle of Spiritual Discernment

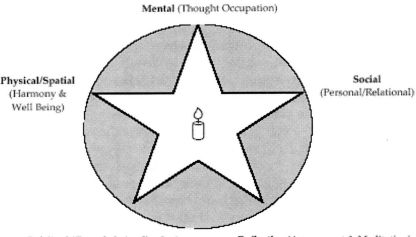

Mental (Thought Occupation)

Physical/Spatial (Harmony & Well Being)

Social (Personal/Relational)

Spiritual (Growth & Application)

Reflective (Attunement & Meditation)

The Central Flame – Who You Are and What You Serve

In its introduction, there was one aspect of *The Pentacle of Spiritual Discernment* that I did not explain which is the single candle situated in its middle. Before I explain this candle's significance, I would like to make an assertion about the material and non-material aspects of our lives. I believe our life is an altar. Through the very gesture of living day after day and year after year, we build and maintain the altar of our lives. This altar is a reflection of who we choose to be. As such, it is our sacred offering back to spirit, the living world and humanity. Our life as an altar has two aspects: its material contents and its nonmaterial contents. The material contents of our altar consist of the physical aspects of our lives; they are the actions and deeds that can be seen or witnessed by others. The material aspect of my altar contains things like female, teacher, seer, ritualist, environmental economist, cook and poet to name a few. The non-material contents of our altar consist of the thought-forms and cultivated consciousness of our inner life. These aspects of our altar are detectible but not visible to others; they are, however, visible to the beings of adjacent worlds. The non-material contents of my altar includes my daily meditations, my beliefs, what I think but do not say, my heart's desires, how I treat myself and my approach to the world. If we think of our life as an altar, every thought, act, meditation and deed becomes an object upon it. And as we know, an altar draws matter and energy to its field of influence as well as dispels matter and energy from its field of influence. When we think of our lives as an altar, we realize that anything we think or do becomes part and parcel of who we are. Contrary to what we may have believed before, it is not just our physical deeds and actions that we should care about in our endeavor to live an admirable life. Our innermost thoughts that radiate outward from our core drawing to us similar reflections, qualities and circumstances should share our concern as well. By the same token, it is not enough to focus on our meditations and ritual practices in an effort to live a spiritually amiable life. Our outward actions and deeds radiate from within us drawing to us similar reflections, qualities and circumstances. We all know people who go to church on Sunday, gain the approval of their spiritual community and then yell at their children or engage in acts of marital infidelity during the week. The mindset that perpetuates this kind of visible versus invisible compartmentalization is one of the greatest fallacies we can create in our lives. Some think they can categorize themselves and their lives into the acts and deeds that are seen versus those that are unseen. Others think that even if their lives are incongruent, if they pray for forgiveness, it is ok if their actions don't really change. Never are these silly rationalizations reflective of any real and abiding spiritual truth. If we are to live our lives as men and women of spirit we must realize that the whole of our lives is the weight and measure that counts. Our life is indeed an altar, consisting of the seen and unseen, public and private aspects of ourselves. In the center of this altar, amidst all the seen and unseen aspects we find a single, central flame. This is the flame that resides within the heart of *The Pentacle of Spiritual Discernment.* A description of its place and purpose follows.

In ancient temples, a central fire was tended day and night by Priests and Priestesses dedicated to this task. In the not-so-distant past, home hearth fires were tended carefully with the same kind of love and devotion. For centuries, ceremonies and rituals of all cultures have had fire or a flame as the central focus of a sacred circle. The sanctity of the central fire has been part and parcel of our lives for thousands of years. As long as the flames were tended, the being(s) for which they burned remained in close contact to the guardians of the flame. The single, central flame in the center of *The Pentacle of Spiritual Discernment* is like these sacred fires; it is the light we kindle when we come into this life. Its illumination casts a warm, guiding glow on all that we think, feel, do and become. Whether or not we realize it, this central fire burns in honor of that to which we dedicate our inner and outer life. Throughout our lives we tend this flame. Day after day, we continue to care for and be led by its glow until the time comes to extinguish this life's light and evolve forward. I call this unique inner light the *Central Flame*. The *Central Flame* is the spiritual fire that burns in the core of our being. Because it illuminates and radiates the force of all our thoughts, deeds and actions, it is our personal "holy of holies." It codifies our pact with the spiritual forces with whom we are aligned. The *Central Flame* burns in remembrance of the dedication of our life; it is our soul's covenant. It is the inward point from which all outer expressions of our self and our Self[48] spring forth. And its light glows upon and guides all five points of *The Pentacle of Spiritual Discernment*. Now that we understand the impetus for this light, let us journey forward in a discussion of how the *Central Flame* functions and can assist us in our practice of spiritual discernment.

---

[48] In PCA we often refer to the little "s" self and the big "S" Self. The self consists of our simple human consciousness that engages with the mundane aspects of life, finding itself attached to the story and the human drama of life. The Self consists of our elevated human consciousness that engages with the esoteric aspects of life, finding itself attached to the myth and the spiritual truths of the greater good. Both are necessary when living a human life, the trick is to realize when and where to live from these places and how to merge them appropriately.

One of the most important protections against being a source or vessel of psychic disturbance is to maintain and live by your core principles. If you know where you end and the rest of the universe begins, you will have established a key boundary to keep yourself and others safe. [49] – Caitlín Matthews

Since the start of PCA in 1999, we've repeated one question over and over again to our students, "Who are you?" We ask this at our annual initiation ritual and the beginning of each class day. We ask this before and after our rites of passage and at the threshold of our annual closing ceremony. Since the beginning of PCA the question "Who are you?" has been our crossroads inquiry. To our physical body system and to the unseen worlds, the answers given in response to this question confirm our choices and alignments as men and women of spirit. When faced with the ubiquitous soul searching questions like "Who am I"? or "What am I doing here?" men and women of spirit must always know the answer. We must know who we are at the core, we must know what spiritual forces we allow to work through us, and we must know how to align with those forces within seconds and in any given situation.

From the beginning, second year PCA students have been tasked with crafting a personal statement which clearly and concisely declares their alignments as a man or woman of spirit. Comparatively, we've asked our third year students to fashion a Covenant that clearly and concisely articulates their service, spiritual alignments and commitments beyond graduation. The message I've quoted from Caitlín Matthew's *The Psychic Protection Handbook* is an extremely important one. After reading her book, I realized that we were remiss waiting until the second year of ceremonial study to ask our students to know and declare who they are. This clarity of self and purpose must be one of the first acts men and women of spirit perform when deepening their spiritual and magical abilities. Thus we added a third component of the "Who are you?" inquiry to our program which compels our first year students to write and declare their own *Central Flame* statement. Today this statement serves as

---

[49] Matthews, Caitlín. *The Psychic Protection Handbook*, Piatkus Books Ltd, London, Great Britain, 2005, pp 14.

the spiritual foundation for their first and second year of study. During their third year, each student expands their *Central Flame* statement into a personal Covenant which illuminates and guides their spiritual work after PCA.

In both the mundane and spiritual aspects of our life, often it is the obvious and simple teachings that are the most profound. In search of some greater complexity we frequently look to a far horizon when instead the answer rests squarely at our feet. In the current pursuit, we are very much concerned with our feet for it is our feet that tell us where we stand. The probing inquiries of the "Who are you?" genre are all based upon the premise that before we learn which spiritual forces we should say "no" to, we must first determine which spiritual forces we say "yes" to. When we clearly and concisely determine our spiritual alignments and commitments, we are better equipped to recognize and reject what we know to be "other." If we know who we are, what we stand for, with what spiritual forces we are aligned, we are a clearer and more stable practitioner. When a vessel is empty, it invites occupancy. If the vessel of our spiritual core is not occupied by our own will and intention, it appears "open" and by this virtue invites occupancy. If, on the other hand, our spiritual core is full with our own will and intention, we have less available space to attract uninvited guests. If we are not clear as to who we are and whom or what we serve, we are malleable. When we are malleable, it is easier for subtle forces to permeate, delude and influence us.

Though parts of us must remain truly flexible and able to flow with the inevitable changes to our life's assumed course, our ethical, moral and spiritual core must be inflexible and resistant to corruption.

That which you consider to be the core of your very existence should be well rooted within your consciousness so as to ward off that which seeks to challenge and undermine you. Thus in PCA we train our students to have an immediate answer to "Who am I?", in the form of a *Central Flame* statement, so that when they find themselves in sticky situations this knowledge of self is automatically engaged within them. Anything you may need to employ in a moment of stress, pressure or panic should be practiced when times are clear and spaces safe. As a mundane example: when I drive, I occasionally practice exactly what I intend to do if a tire on my car suddenly gives out. In my mind, I think "bang...

the tire goes!" Next I think "foot off gas, turn on hazard lights and pull over to the side of the road." I've even set these words to a little tune in my mind. One icy winter day, I was driving myself and a friend over a traffic-congested and icy mountain road. Suddenly a tire on my car exploded. The little song I created kicked in automatically. I did not even have to think about it, it just happened as I had rehearsed it fifty times before. In this sudden shift of events, my little mantra enabled me to safely escort myself and my passenger off the road without causing an accident. When our spiritual muscles are exercised and strengthened on a routine basis, they will self-activate and hold firm when we need them.

> *If we have linked our mortally manifested lives properly with this highest self-point, then it will naturally operate to some degree at this level also. So, when faced by the evil this world might amass, let us know inside ourselves that we can more than out match it in the spiritual states of self it can never overcome while we intend otherwise.* [50] – W. G. Gray

Take a moment to stop and read the preceding quotation from W. G. Gray once more. It says when we link ourselves with the highest self point; we will naturally operate in a manner that is not restricted by the trials and tribulations of our lower self. Further, when we do face that which this or another world might throw at us, we can more than outmatch it if we are clear in our intentions and alliances. When we interact with the beings and energies of the unseen worlds, we must be very clear who we are, what we stand for and who our spiritual allies are in force and form. As was the case with my car tire scenario, we may need this information on a moment's notice. If we panic or flail in these instances, we open ourselves to otherworldly influences that can confuse, misdirect and potentially harm us. Knowing who we are creates the set of laws or principles by which we operate. These laws or principles attract and disperse the experiences, teachings, health effects, spiritual paths, friends, children and lovers of our lives. In this day and age of quantum spirituality, words like "attract" and "dispel" sound quite familiar. Though perhaps it possesses them, the *Central Flame* was not conceived upon quantum principles. It is instead conceived

---

[50] Gray, William G. *Exorcising the Tree of Evil*, Kima Global Publishers, Cape Town South Africa 2002, pg.199-200.

upon the foundational belief that it is a soul's choice to evolve, incarnate, experience life, give, receive, learn and grow. As such, the *Central Flame* is a continuation of the greater work and codes to which the soul and the human vessel it manifests are both bound. When we know who we are and we state that to the seen and unseen worlds, we fill our vessel with will and intention. We create a field of resonance within us that defines and emanates the particular frequency that we define as our Self. When we know who we are it is much easier to discern who we are not. Further, as we beam a particular quality of light and sound from our physical body system in the form of our *Central Flame*, we can detect "other" with a greater degree of knowledge and accuracy. With this in mind, let us turn our attention to the creation and declaration of your *Central Flame* statement.

When you initiate the process of creating a personal *Central Flame*, it is helpful to begin by exploring the feeling tones of your being through meditation and soft exploration. In other words, don't immediately put pen to paper to compose the ultimate statement of your life without any forethought. Spend time asking yourself a few leading questions such as "Who am I?" or "Who walks with me from the unseen worlds?" For some, creating a *Central Flame* statement may flow quickly and easily as the personal life dedication is clear and unwavering. For others, this inquiry may seem challenging at first and require considerable time, which is fine. Sometimes when posed with questions such as these, we can feel intimidated and thus become stuck in the contemplation. Often we simply live our lives engaged in our self, yet unconscious of the Self we also are. Even if you feel you know your *Central Flame* statement immediately, contemplate it for a while; reflect upon each aspect of it until you are absolutely certain it is right for you. During this contemplation, focus upon the following five inquiries until you are certain you have considered all aspects pertinent to the formation of this statement.

1.   To what work or avocation have I been drawn most consistently? What do I feel is my service and contribution to offer into the worlds (seen and unseen)?

2.   What "myths" do I seem to be living in this life and how have they unfolded for me?

3.   How do my personal oracles inform my life's mission? (e.g. astrological chart, numerology, enneagram, tarot readings, spiritual intuitive reading etc.) Note: In doing this level of in-

quiry, please rely on time-tested oracles as opposed to the inauthentic oracles permeating the new-age marketplace.

4. What brings me the greatest and most pure sense of soul derived joy and fulfillment?

5. In whose Name(s) do I walk and who, in turn, guides me along my path?

After you have contemplated these five points of inquiry, combine your answers into one large paragraph that includes all information referenced. From here, pare down this larger paragraph into its essence. Your aim is to craft a *Central Flame* statement that is no longer than that which is convenient to commit to memory. This statement must be memorized; no exceptions. Further, though the particulars may be your own, the *Central Flame* must always include these two things: 1) What I choose to do with the life force granted me and 2) In whose Name I offer my Self and service as a man or women of spirit. The first point is the spoken commitment of an intentional life. Rather than including the particulars of what you do, let it reflect the essence of who you are. For instance, instead of saying "I am a teacher, healer, mother and friend," which is quite nebulous, one would say "I offer compassion and listener's ear to all who cross my path as teacher, healer, mother and friend." Simply listing your occupation says nothing about what of yourself you give to the effort. The second point regarding "in whose Name" may need a little clarification.

When we create a statement that sets forth our soul's intention in being here, it is important to reestablish our individual connection to the spiritual forces of the adjacent worlds. The term "spiritual forces" includes but is not limited to the following commonly used terms: angelic forces, faery contacts, spirit allies or guides, inner contacts, supreme beings, everlasting qualities and benevolent ancestral spirits. Inside our religious tradition or spiritual practice, we work with spiritual forces that are aligned with our particular path. This is one of the reasons why the New Age phenomenon of path shopping is a concern for many spiritual teachers. I work as a minister of a transdenominational temple that serves many different religious traditions and spiritual lifestyles[51]. In this capacity, I have come to

---

[51] I chose the phrase "religion traditions or spiritual lifestyles" purposefully out of respect for the practices, such as Hinduism or Native American traditions, that do not consider themselves a religion but instead a way of living and being.

believe that each religion or tradition is a spoke upon the Wheel of Life. Each spoke of the Wheel is blessed with particular spiritual energies and beings that partner with humans toward the mutual fulfillment of the gift or purpose of that particular tradition. Thus bestowed and aligned, each spoke of the Wheel has a part to play in the greater evolution. For instance, I appreciate Jainism as the spoke of nonviolent victory over inner enemies to birth our higher qualities, Buddhism as the spoke of enlightenment and release from suffering and Christianity as the spoke of brotherhood and sisterhood toward redemption. The hub of the Wheel of Life is the Universal, all-encompassing principle of Divine Unity, inseparable by faith, gender or culture.

When we choose to walk our true path and enliven our chosen spoke, we assist in the strengthening of the Wheel toward the unity of all faiths and peoples. Each tradition is equipped with particular spiritual forces that possess specific capacities for working in the fields of resonance created by that tradition. When we perform the work unique to any one spiritual tradition, we align with the unseen beings that exist within it. If we path shop, we end up mixing spiritual traditions and their attendant spiritually aligned beings in a way that dilutes spiritual power. Though it can be tempting to mix and match (especially in a world that needs to increase its respect for spiritual and cultural diversity), in determining the Name(s) in which you offer your service, it will serve you best and most fully to choose one spoke...one path. From here look to the most exalted spiritual forces within this particular religious tradition or spiritual lifestyle that are best suited for the way you choose to employ your life energy. If, for example, your *Central Flame* statement directs your life energy toward guiding and mentoring young children as an elementary schoolteacher, then you might call upon the light, lance and uprightness of Archangel Michael to be the Name and spiritual stream into which you offer your service. If your life's work is dedicated to assisting troubled couples by providing marriage counseling, then you might call upon the power and grace of Sacred Union of Divine Masculine and Divine Feminine forces to be the Names and spiritual stream into which you offer your service. In making these alliances, it is important to realize that it is not that these deities become attached to us as individuals for, as we have stated before, their focus is planetary and cosmic not individualized. Instead, by virtue of aligning our service to their particular spiritual resonance, we attune to the stream of power that they mediate into the world and as such are graced by the host of spiritual beings that work within that particular stream. This connection informs the transpersonal elements of our spiritual practices and becomes the "Oversoul" of our life's work and sacred service. It is the presence, power and guidance of this stream (e.g. the stream of Archangel Michael, the Divine Mother or Sacred Union) that guides, works with and through you as the oversoul of your *Central Flame*. As we determine in whose Name(s) we offer our service, be mindful of your chosen spoke of the Wheel and the spiritual beings that hover there in benevolent service to the gift or purpose of your sacred way of knowing and living. Finally, please also note that few of us begin and end our conscious service as a man or woman of spirit in exactly the same manner. Most of us find that, due to the impact of the spiritual and personal work we perform, the specifics of our service shift and change as our consciousness shifts and changes. When and if we find ourselves occupying a new and different spiritual or personal service to the worlds, it is appropriate to revisit our *Central Flame* statement. If and when we alter this statement, we may also need to alter our Oversoul (e.g. in whose Name) alliances appropriately.

Once you have constructed your *Central Flame* statement and determined your Oversoul, it is important that you perform a personal ritual of proclamation. When ritualizing your statement keep these two intentions in mind, 1) placing your *Central Flame* statement squarely in the physical and metaphysical realms as an imprint, and 2) affirming your spiritual alliances. When you ritualize your *Central Flame* statement, do so in the manner of your choice. The ritual can be as simple or as elaborate as you choose. Be sure that you purify yourself, create your sacred sphere, speak your intention and spend some time in quiet reception of the spiritual forces that you are calling to you. The culminating act of any *Central Flame* ritual is the lighting of a physical candle that symbolically represents your Central Flame and its place in the center of *The Pentacle of Spiritual Discernment*. As you do this, speak your statement aloud and call to the spiritual forces in whose Name you offer your Self as the Oversoul of your work and purpose. As with any ritual of declaration, the key is to offer your *Central Flame* statement and request the assistance of your chosen allies with complete sincerity. Before you release your sacred sphere and close the ritual, spend a little time calling into focus and assessing the seen and unseen contents of your life altar. Let the light of your newly lit *Central Flame* illuminate each item you have placed there over time. Take stock of the deeds and actions of your external world and the thoughts, reflections and contemplations of your internal world. Reinforce each item you feel pleased to keep on your life altar. Remove each item you feel it is time to release. In your journal, record a clear reflection of what you experienced during this ritual, what you observed on your life altar, what you choose to continue placing there and what you choose to remove. From here, release the ritual elements and return to your outer world awareness. Now you are ready to tend your *Central Flame* through your personal spiritual practices as well as the choices and actions of your life. The *Central Flame* is as organic as you are, thus will likely shift and change slightly over days, weeks and years to come. Each time you make a significant change to your statement, ritualize the statement anew. Stay current with your own process and progress; stay awake in the sacred co-creation of your life.

To complete this section I offer my own *Central Flame* statement. *"As Priestess and Celtic Woman, I dedicate myself to the remembrance and reemergence of the Divine Feminine, to weaving seen and unseen worlds in harmony, balance and mutual respect and to the furtherance of the Western Esoteric Tradition. I do so in the Name of the Sacred Union of the Divine Father and Divine Mother."*

Develop and Consistently Tend
Your Relationships with Spiritual Forces

> *The antigens to ills caused by evil are derived from our deepest self-levels coming into close contact with divinity...no competent priest of any faith or initiate of any spiritual system would expect for one instant to exorcise even mild evils purely by their personal powers alone.* [52] – W. G. Gray

Thus far in the Methods and Application section, we have performed a personal observation of our lifestyle and spiritual

---

[52] Gray, William G. *Exorcising the Tree of Evil*, Kima Global Publishers, Cape Town South Africa 2002, p. 200, 201.

habits which allowed us to honestly assess the starting point of our spiritual discernment practice. We have also determined, written and ritualized our *Central Flame* statement. In doing so we either created or reaffirmed our alliance with the spiritual forces to which we pay the greatest homage by virtue of our chosen sacred service as men and women of spirit. From here, we must engage in the third aspect of a spiritual discernment practice by fully turning our attention toward developing and tending our relationships with these benevolent beings of the adjacent worlds. To some persons reading this book, a working relationship between humans and spirit allies, guides or inner contacts is part and parcel of their lives. To others, a working relationship with the spiritual forces is a concept they understand, but do not know how to put into practice in a real and meaningful way. It is for these persons that I write this section which consists of our third step in building a personal spiritual discernment practice.

How Our Alliance with Benevolent Spiritual Forces Assists Us

Near the beginning of this book, I offered a quotation from Rudolph Steiner that speaks to the fact that spirit beings belong to and operate in their world just as human beings belong to and operate in our world. The message in this quote can seem one-dimensional at first blush; however, with time and experience its true depth is revealed. In addition to pointing out the obvious division of the worlds, Steiner also offers insight into the rules of engagement which govern the interactions between spirit beings and human beings. Here is an example from the physical world that expands and clarifies this assertion.

One of my mentors, Doug Jones, offered this analogy to me when explaining the importance of our knowing and working intimately with spiritual forces. Let us consider the two vastly different games of water polo and American football. Both games demand a great deal of strength and skill; however, each requires very different equipment. If a football player adorned with layers of padding, a helmet and shoes were to step into a water polo game, no amount of skill or strength in football would keep him from being extremely ineffective in a pool of water. By the same token, a half-naked water polo player would not survive for long on the football field were he to be tackled by a fully padded, helmet-wearing defensive lineman. Though most of the ethical principles extend across the divide between the worlds, we must realize that the playing fields of the physical and non-physical worlds are completely different and thus require different equipment. The deeper meaning to Steiner's quote is revealed in this example. Human and spirit beings not only live in distinct worlds, they are naturally "equipped" to function best within their respective worlds as well. When touring a foreign country, whose language we do not speak and customs we do not understand, it can be exceedingly helpful to hire someone from that country to guide us on our travels. Likewise, when venturing into the adjacent worlds, it is most helpful to have a spiritual guide along for whom the place we venture is home. Not only do our spiritual guides enable us to better navigate the unseen worlds by virtue of their familiarity, they assist us to acquire and develop the right otherworldly "equipment" which fortifies our spiritual and magical work. The *opportunity* to journey back and forth across the veil comes to us in many natural forms (e.g. meditation, dreams, visions, ritual, etc.) However the *ability* to safely journey there and back requires special skills and aptitudes. To effectively work in the otherworlds, we must gradually and increasingly cultivate a capacity for doing so with clarity of purpose and perception.

The first skill and aptitude we must cultivate within ourselves is an ability to extend our consciousness into the inner worlds. I have mentioned this before and will likely do so again; for men and women of spirit our consciousness is our greatest tool. We may possess a dozen consecrated sacred objects, have memorized all the right incantations and own beautiful ritual attire, but if we cannot employ our consciousness to part the veils and connect to the power of the primal worlds authentically; we may as well offer all our spiritual accoutrements to The Salvation Army. If we wish to safely journey back and forth between the worlds, we must develop the conditions of consciousness that permit and promote this work. This involves routinely engaging in appropriately-calibrated meditative and ritual practices which enable us to clear our minds of the daily clutter and truly and effectively engage with particular inner world alliances. The development of our consciousness in this manner requires repetition, because through repetition we hone skills and build capacities. The repetition of which I speak is not dissimilar to the discipline through which an athlete develops and maintains his or her strength and ability. Repetition of the right physical exercises, in the right order, combined with meticulous eating, sleeping and thinking create the foundation from which an athlete may excel to the best of his or her ability. If any aspect of this regime is compromised the performance will also be compromised. The same is true of men and women of spirit.

The second skill and ability required to safely journey into the otherworlds and back is the cultivation and maintenance of relationships with the spiritual forces of these worlds who act as guides and mentors for us. Continuing our sports metaphor, these working partnerships are similar to relationship between an athlete and his or her coach. The coach, who has been through the rigors of the sport, knows how to increase the physical capacity and sporting ability of the novice. By the same token, it is important for a spiritual novice to solicit the assistance of spiritual forces, guides, guardians and inner contacts. These beings guide us into, direct us within and assist us to exit our otherworldly engagements. They also help us avoid malevolent beings because their orientation to these negative/retarding forces is must more direct and tangible relative to our own. Just as a water polo player meeting his football player friend prior to a match would be sure he was properly suited for an aquatic sport, spiritual forces guide and advise us in ways that ensure our safety in the unfamiliarity of the otherworlds. Finally, just as a strong and positively situated group of friends can keep us from mingling with the wrong crowds, spiritual companions bolster our own inner resonance, which deflects otherworldly harm or injury from our physical body system. In other words, the very presence and resonance of benevolent inner contacts, guides and guardians provides a quality of association that the less exalted or malevolent beings seek to avoid.

Before moving on, it should be clearly understood that the relationship between us and our spiritual forces was never designed to be a one way street. The spiritual forces are not here simply to serve us; they have tasks and duties of their own to fulfill. Some of which have a direct effect on the physical world and its inhabitants. Just as we need their assistance to accomplish our work, the spiritual forces we work with often require the assistance of their human partners to accomplish their work as well. Thus, at times our otherworldly partners will ask us to assist them. Our willingness to do so in the spirit of reciprocity strengthens the bonds of our mutually, beneficial companionship.

How Do We Begin?

The spiritual forces who reside within the adjacent worlds know the otherworldly territories better than we can with our strongly physical orientations. Because of this, in matters of spiritual defense they are invaluable. Many, if not all of us have some sense of the spiritual forces with whom we are able to commune. However, I have found that a disproportionately small number of people actively practicing spiritual and magical arts make the time to develop these connections to the point where they truly know how to work well with an otherworldly ally. In my experience this underdevelopment tends to be a function of two personal attributes: spiritual lassitude and spiritual uncertainty.

Many spiritual practitioners possess the technical "know how" but lack the inner fortitude to tend to their otherworldly alliances. Persons such as this attend workshops, belong to spiritual associations, read dozens of esoteric texts and can truly "talk the talk", yet when it comes to actually applying all of the knowledge they have accumulated, they lack the inner will and discipline to put it into practice. You will remember from the Foundations and Definitions section of this book that the first principle of personal responsibility with regard to a spiritual discernment practice was realizing that only we, and we alone, can build our spiritual muscles. Without continuously repeating the techniques we've learned that enable us to commune and build alliances with our otherworldly allies, we cannot do so. In search of the spiritual high that results from the occasional glorious ritual or meditative experience, these days many people are drawn by the power and mystique of the spiritual world. Some of these seekers will actually find themselves committing to the deeper practices which, over time, enable them to become true men or women of spirit. The rest will find ways to engage in the "feel good" experiences of occasional otherworldly contacts, but will not exert themselves on their own behalf toward the mastery of this art form. This is the scenario to which I refer when using the term spiritual lassitude. It refers to those people who dabble but never really commit. Let us now move on to a description of the scenario referred to as spiritual uncertainty.

Some practitioners sincerely wish to cultivate reliable other-worldly relationships. They engage in the same kinds of classes, meditations, preparatory exercises and associations but when it comes right down to it, they feel lost and confused when faced with the task of grounding or incorporating their esoteric experiences and knowledge into their daily lives. Often for these people personal work done on their own, away from a teacher or peers, feels like a big undertaking with too many unknowns. Where those harboring the attributes of spiritual lassitude are simply too languid and unfocused to engage in the discipline of a repetitious spiritual practice, persons hampered by spiritual uncertainty lack a sense of personal confidence and trust. They are sincere in their desire, yet they simply don't possess the individual will forces that are necessary to overcome the weight and uncertainty of it all. All too often these people consistently look outside themselves for verification, choosing to give away their personal, spiritual power versus risk trusting themselves as wise enough to go it alone.

Somewhere along the way, most if not all of us have found ourselves facing spiritual lassitude, spiritual uncertainty or both. When we find ourselves navigating these places within us, the trick is to recognize this inertia and work to shift it before we find ourselves lying flat on our back, clobbered by a defensive lineman while wearing our swimming suit and goggles. In other words, these two occupations of spiritual mis-application can, if left unchecked, steer us out of our spiritual depths before we know it. Similar to the perils suffered by the infamous "weekend warrior", without a steadily attending to and building of our spiritual muscles and otherworldly alliances, we may think we can go from weeks of inertia to weekends of full-on spiritual exertion, no problem. Rarely, if ever, is this the case. Thus the true answer to the question "How do we begin?" which initiated this subsection, is to actually assess our own places of spiritual lassitude and uncertainty. To do this we must evaluate ourselves honestly, by determining our readiness to set aside incompatible personal tendencies in favor of cultivating true and enduring otherworldly alliances as a man or woman of spirit. When this is done, we are better able to develop a personal spiritual practice that fosters right relationships between ourselves and our allies in the unseen worlds; there is no other way.

Developing and Working with Objective and Subjective Personal Cross Check Systems

In the Foundations and Definitions section of this book I discussed the importance of setting up objective and subjective systems in an effort to lessen our tendencies toward the pitfalls of illusion and false egoism. Because our spiritual discernment work is now orienting strongly toward tending our otherworldly relationships, and work of this nature is vulnerable to illusive and egotistical influences, it is important to speak more about these systems.

Personal cross check systems enable us to double check our orientation to and interpretations of the unseen worlds. Objective systems of spiritual cross checking consist of the less opaque methods that men and women of spirit can use to assess the genuineness of their own spiritual intuitions or inspirations. These methods include consulting an oracle, our body's wisdom or a trusted friend to double check the accuracy and reliability or our spiritual intuitions. Subjective systems rely upon our personal foundations in meditation and dream work to advise us in the same manner. The concept behind the use of objective and subjective personal cross check systems is quite simple. When we receive spiritual guidance, intuition or inspiration and we are unclear as to the accuracy or reliability of the information itself and/or our interpretations, we employ an objective or subjective assessment tool to double check ourselves. At the start I would like to say that over the years I have found that more often than not, the initial guidance, inspiration or intuition received by men and women of spirit is fairly accurate. More often than not, it is our mental or emotional filters that are responsible for skewing the information we receive from our unseen allies. For example, if we are generally pessimistic we can possess a tendency to skew spiritual information in generally cynical or distrustful direction; the reverse can be true of optimists. Likewise, we might receive information we simply don't want to hear because it asks something of us we would rather not give; in these instances we may skew information away from the obvious truth and toward the conclusion we prefer. Because we possess these tendencies, it is often advisable to cross check our intuitions and intuitive interpretations via objective methods, subjective methods or both. At the start, it is best to work with the objective systems as they rely upon less obscure means of cross checking ourselves. In this spirit, let us begin with a discussion of the objective methods known as divination, collegial corroboration and bodily wisdom.

When working with the divination method, I recommend students use well founded oracles such as the traditional Tarot, I Ching or Runes[53]. I have personally found many of the "dime-a-dozen" contemorary oracles to be less well founded and thus inappropriate for these deeper, spiritual purposes. Unfortunately, the modern world of oracles has become populated by divination means and methods that were contrived for purely financial gain. I always do my best to steer our students away from thinly-composed spiritual oracles in favor of those with deeper, esoteric foundations. To use divination as your cross check, simply perform a personal reading by asking the oracle a question such as "What meets me if I interpret and follow this spiritual guidance in this manner?" or "What is the spiritual impulse behind this guidance?" The oracle's answer to your question will help to condone or correct the guidance, inspiration or intuition at hand.

Alternately you may double check yourself by seeking a second opinion from a trusted brother or sister who is also engaged in spiritual and magical work, and is at least as advanced, if not more advanced, than yourself. To use this method, present the inspiration, guidance or intuition you've received and the circumstances of its coming to your friend. From here ask them to extend their otherworldly senses on your behalf in pursuit of additional clarity that double checks your intuitions. Again questions like, "What meets me if follow this spiritual guidance in this fashion?" or "What meets me if do not follow this spiritual guidance in this fashion?" are most helpful in this regard.

Finally, you may also learn to rely upon the calibrated wisdom of your own body as a means for checking the accuracy of your spiritual inspirations and guidance. *The Body Barometer* ex-

---

[53] The Viking and Germanic Runes available for purchase today are not what one would call traditional, in that the ancient use of Runes was much different. According to Edred Thorsson, author of *Futhark: A Handbook of Rune Magick*, runes were incantations, not letters painted on rocks or burned into wood. Nevertheless, I find this oracle's roots quite available through their contemporary use and thus continue to recommend them. Someone seriously interested in the traditional use of Runes may wish to engage in the work of Thorrsson and other similar scholars.

ercise put forth earlier is the tool I use to gauge my inner sage's response to my own intuitive interpretations. In this situation as before, scan your body in search of its wisdom center on this day. From here ask it to reflect to you through sensation, image or temperature what meets you if you follow this spiritual guidance. Once received, clear this feedback and then ask it to reflect what meets you if you do not.

Once you have developed a muscle for accurate self reflection based upon the objective personal cross check methods, you can begin to work with the subjective personal cross check methods. Again, subjective methods rely upon our own personal foundations in meditation and dream work to advise us. If our foundations are not strong and clear, the information received can be skewed by the interpretative filters we've not yet learned to recognize in ourselves. For this reason, subjective personal cross check methods should only be used by practitioners who are relatively certain of the integrity of their sacred imagination and are thus not recommended for newer practitioners. Because they are perhaps less well known than the objective methods, I will discuss the subjective personal cross check methods in some detail.

When uncertain as to the quality and integrity of your own spiritual inspiration, guidance or intuition, it can be very helpful to enter into a discerning meditation. One must be very clear when utilizing discerning meditations for they are subject to conjecture if one's sacred imagination is not well calibrated. If we have any unhealthy or illusive filters in place, they may color the results of this meditation.

Cross Check Meditation

Begin by lighting a candle mindful of your intention. Cast a sacred sphere around yourself and then call to your personal guides and guardians for assistance. Employ your sacred imagination to recall in detail the spiritual guidance, inspiration or intuition you are questioning. Holding this recollection clearly within your mind and heart, now ask: "What meets me if follow this spiritual guidance in this fashion?" or "What meets me if do not follow this spiritual guidance in this fashion?" From here, open all your otherworldly senses to receive information in response to this question from your inner contacts. In essence, the quality of the inner and/or otherworldly response you receive in relationship to this question indicates the appropriate course of action or inaction as the case may be. In response, you can expect to see, sense, hear or feel the imprints or impressions of each course of action as you are permitted and able to perceive them. If, upon asking this question, you see, hear, feel or know vitality in the form of warmth, light, brightness or encouragement then you may trust the guidance, inspiration or intuition in question is genuine and rightly interpreted by you. If instead, you see, hear, feel or know a vital energy drain in the form of cold, dark, dullness or resistance then you are best served by stepping back from this guidance, inspiration or intuition for something is amiss.

There is another question that can aid men and women of spirit engaged in a subjective cross check inquiry: "As I am allowed to witness and able to perceive, what is the spiritual power behind X?" I would like to point out that this question is extremely helpful to men and women of spirit who are learning how to develop trusted otherworldly instincts. Its use is founded upon the belief that when a bond of mutual respect has been formed between the human practitioner and his or her guides and guardians, they can and will offer direct feedback in inquiries such as these. In its posing, we are asking to see, sense, hear or feel the spiritual power or force behind (or motivating) the intuition or inspiration in question. Because it relies upon the calibration of our sacred imagination, it should only be used by practitioners who have spent the time building strong relationships with their otherworldly guides and guardians. When you ask this question of your otherworldly allies, do so respectfully, for you are being given a precious view or sense of the unseen. The phrase "as I am allowed to witness and able to perceive" is an important aspect of this meditation as it allows for the appropriate tailoring of the message as discerned by your spiritual guides and inner contacts. Consequently, two people doing this exercise together may see, sense, hear or feel slightly different specific expressions of the power behind X; however, the tone and theme of the information obtained should be consistent.

Now let us move on to the dream state method. This method relies upon the feedback offered to you by the unseen realms through the experience of dream invocation. In essence, the practitioner goes to sleep in a particular fashion and with a specific intention to receive otherworldly guidance reflective of their understanding of a spiritual directive, intuition or inspiration. To work with the dream state, begin by purifying yourself and your sleeping quarters appropriately, thus removing any imprints that could impinge upon the quality of your sleeping and dreaming. If purification as a sacred art form is new to you, advance ahead to the section titled "Develop and Maintain a Practice of Spiritual-Physical Hygiene." Its contents will assist you in deciding how best to purify yourself and your sleeping quarters for this work. Once the purification of your sleeping quarters is complete, cast a sacred sphere that encompasses yourself and your sleeping quarters; then call to your guardian and any other appropriate inner contacts. From here, speak aloud your sincere desire to receive clarity with regard to the spiritual inspiration, intuition or guidance in question. Bring your consciousness into a state of stillness; then allow yourself to fall asleep as you normally would. The quality of sleep and dreams that follow composes the answer to your question. If you experience a peaceful and inspired night, or perhaps receive confirming dream images, then you may trust that following this inspiration, intuition or guidance itself and your interpretations of it is advised for your highest good. If, on the other hand, you experience a stressful and static night, or perhaps receive troublesome dream images, then you are best served releasing this inspiration, intuition or guidance and/or your current interpretations of it for something within the guidance or your interpretation of it is amiss.

With the basics of objective and subjective personal cross check systems in place, we can now move forward into the aspects of the spiritual discernment practice that requires us to determine, form and maintain our relationships with the benevolent beings and energies of the unseen worlds most appropriate for us and our work.

It Is Up To Us To Call Them Forth

If we wish to work successfully with the benevolent spiritual forces of adjacent worlds, we must understand that for the most part, they are not self-initiating beings. Nearly always, spiritual forces come only when sincerely summoned. To receive their grace and strength we must call their names and open to feel their presence beyond any tendencies toward fear or confusion. This is not to say that our spirit allies never assert themselves on our behalf; in times of great struggle or challenge they will do so without a direct request. Yet we must understand these particular engagements (e.g. near death, accidents, danger, trauma, child birth, etc.) are based upon past soul agreements and are, fortunately, rare in the scope of a human life. By and large, our day-to-day work with the unseen world is based upon matters and factors that are far less grave than those that constitute an unsolicited intervention. Additionally, it is always up to us to do our part to take care of ourselves through proper employment of our spiritual and magical capabilities. Again, our relationship with our allies of the unseen worlds is a two way street; they will do their part to assist us and we must employ our will and attentions to do our part to assist ourselves as well. As has already been established, the spiritual forces with whom we work have their own tasks and duties that occupy them just as our general tasks and duties occupy us.

To begin this process, we must figure out our own right associations in the unseen worlds. In other words, we must determine which quality, deity or guardian force is most apt and fitting to work with us. This is similar to the Name in which we dedicate our *Central Flame* statement and thus should also be compatible with its premise. Most often these alliances are formed from within the pool of spiritual beings and energies associated with the soul alignments of our particular spiritual tradition or stream. In other cases, these alliances seem to be *chosen for us*, versus be *chosen by us* via our particular spiritual affiliations. Often the alliances chosen for us are a function of our biological ancestry or past life associations. Whether our inner allies are chosen by us or for us, it is up to us to meet them and then develop a reliable working relationship with them over time. To begin we must first invite the association. Next, we must make time to cultivate the closeness and reliability that forms a lasting and reliable bond. In forming these relationships always remember that our alliances with the ambassadors of the unseen worlds are constructed upon a basis of mutual consent and respect. When such alliances are formed and bridges of communication built, the spiritual forces can and will assist us in many, many ways. And we, in turn, will likely be asked to assist them in the physical world manifestation of their work. The spiritual forces I work with have done everything from alerting me to something as mundane as how to avoid a potential traffic accident to putting me back together after a hard night of otherworldly combat. After several years of work in this field, I not only know that I *should* never work without the guidance and companionship of my inner contacts and guardian forces, I have weathered enough to realize that I would never *wish* to.

Spiritual Forces Are As Unique As We Are

In beginning this subsection, I would like to speak to some of the interesting observations I have made over the years with regard to humanity's connections to the beings and energies of the otherworlds. In my work as a seer I've noticed two reoccurring patterns that manifest between and among my clients. Year after year I've noticed that without fail there are certain times and/or seasons when requests for intuitive assistance noticeably increase. In addition to the seasonal phenomenon, in many readings spiritual information pertaining to humanity as a whole at that time will come forth for several individuals in succession. To me, these two reoccurring patterns have endearingly reinforced the "oneness" of the human experience. We all live within the same larger ecosystem and are also subject to the same cosmic and planetary alignments, why should we not share our soul work with one another in some way? Each human being is unquestionably unique when viewed from the personal or micro-level. However, when our view widens to the transpersonal or macro-level we amalgamate into one, humanized presence living upon the Earth. It is helpful to remember this as we mature in our spiritual and magical work. We all live on the same planet and are caressed by the same heavenly and earthly imprints; we are thus all subject to a fair amount of common spiritual experiences and information.

On a purely individual level, I've noticed something else of interest. There seems to be a particular pattern woven into the fabric that binds humans and their unseen allies regardless of tradition or orientation. The pattern I see in the individual is related to but slightly different from the collective pattern just mentioned. Through my seership work, I've notice each human client I work with is part of and guided by a particular group or council of spiritual beings and energies that resonate with a common function and purpose. The council is comprised of both the human in physical form and his or her allies in spiritual form. The human and non-human beings on the council are thus co-creatively aligned to serve the advancement of planetary and human consciousness in a unique and particular manner. Although our human and physical countenance distinguishes us from our unseen allies in many ways, all members (human and nonhuman) are equally responsible for contributing to that which the whole council serves as a collective.

It is also important to note that these part human and part nonhuman councils consist of beings and energies with various levels of consciousness and ability; a collection of specialists so to speak. Humans possess particular skills, abilities and capacities that equip and guide us in our aspect of this work. Likewise, the various spiritual beings on our council also possess particular skills, abilities and capacities that direct their work in the inner planes and their interaction with the physical world. As we mature spiritually, it behooves us to learn the nature and character of the spiritual beings and energies that compose our council. As you do you will notice that, by virtue of their specialization, certain beings on our council will step forward at a particular juncture in our lives. These beings are there to assume the lead role during this unique phase or set of circumstances. At the same time, other council beings' presence and participation is relatively constant throughout lives. Situated among the consistently present beings upon our council are the beings I call "guardian spiritual forces." These specialized beings are capable of helping us to maintain our safety and security when encountering the beings and energies of the unseen worlds.

In addition to the core orientation of beings and energies within our council we may also attract other beings and energies to us. As referenced previously, choosing a spiritual path and sticking to it allows the beings and energies associated with that path to work with us clearly and directly. Not doing so can create a muddling of spiritual resonance between the unseen realms and the human realm that is confusing to all. By virtue of our particular contribution to the collective, and thus our council's resonance, many of us are drawn to a particular spiritual path that strengthens and supports us. In the best of circumstances the spiritual path of our choice complements our council's orientation and soul's work. When we choose a particular spiritual path, additional cultural and/or global spiritual allies will be drawn to us. If for instance, your council and thus soul's work best fits within the spiritual path known as Hinduism, once becoming active in this tradition, via its particular meditative and ritual forms, you will serve and be served by the spiritual forces aligned with Hinduism. So although solidly configured, our greater spiritual councils adapt and change somewhat, according to the depth and nature of our spiritual and magical practices. With this in mind, let us augment our appreciation of the spiritual forces with whom we are aligned by exploring methods that enable us to tend and strengthen the relationship between ourselves and the guardian spiritual forces within our council and our chosen spiritual path.

Working With Guardian Spiritual Forces

Earlier I introduced one of my mentors, Doug Jones. In preparation for my first journey to The Holy Land (Israel/Palestine), Doug spoke to me about the importance of developing and tending my relationship with my guardian spiritual forces. I am grateful for the advice that prompted me to pay greater attention to the strength of my relationship to these specialists upon my council. In an effort to foster the same within you, I would like to explore this territory in some depth.

Guardian spiritual forces (hereinafter, guardian) are the beings within our council that possesses the skill and ability to help defend us against the negative/retarding spiritual beings and energies of the adjacent worlds. Guardian spiritual forces may exist in many different forms. Their countenance depends largely upon your particular spiritual tradition and the archetypal imprint of your eternal individuality and soul contracts. To be clear, just like the council of which it is a part, the guardian matches your spiritual tradition, work and associations. For some persons, a guardian manifests as an angelic being that appears cloud-like or geometrical in its form. For others, a guardian manifests in the form of a sacred animal or an amalgamated being of more than one form. As was founded in our earlier discussions, it is important that we do not fantasize the countenance of our guardian by seeing it through the vehicles of a fantasy-impregnated sacred imagination. Guardians come to us in alignment with our spiritual ancestry, biological ancestry or chosen path of deep and committed spiritual application. They are part of our council from either the beginning of our life or the commencement of our chosen spiritual work; our calling to them now merely affirms and strengthens the bonds between us. As an illustration of the point, in most cases, the spirit of the bear does not present itself as a guardian to a practitioner who possesses no specific ancestral or spiritual associations to the peoples and traditions that work with bear medicine. We must surrender to the wisdom of the greater intelligence that guides our spiritual associations versus import our own humanly desires for a guardian in the form of a hulky spiritual warrior or powerful otherworldly lion.

In describing the guardian, I said guardians possess the skill and ability to help defend us against the negative/retarding spiritual beings and energies of the unseen worlds; in this description the phrase "help defend us" is important. A guardian cannot control our lives by whisking us out of danger at every turn, as we are primarily responsible for our own well being. However, it can send direct signals to our physical body system when we are. In their capacity to help defend us, guardians alert us to danger through the inner workings of our primal instincts, emotions and physical sensations. When we are about to encounter a malevolent force of the seen or unseen worlds, guardians will gain our attention by tweaking our physical body system in some recognizable way. Because guardians depend upon our ability to detect and respond to the signals they send to our physical body system, we must spend time learning their language. Now you know why knowing the language of our subtle body has been so greatly emphasized throughout this book.

Like any otherworldly ally, guardians reside and function within the inner realms. To learn their language, we must go partway there to meet them through the practice of focused meditation. During such meditations guardians will teach us the signals they will use to communicate "alert" or "danger" to us. If you are new to this work, it is important to point out that although we may possess a propensity to see and give image-based features to the unseen worlds, where a guardian is concerned it is much more important to develop a *feel* for their presence. If we rely on our sacred imagination as the primary means of communication with our guardians, we may miss the subtle physical and emotional signals they typically send when alerting us to danger.

In addition to helping to alerting us to present concerns, a guardian can teach us about the dangers of the unseen worlds through other forms of meditation when we aren't in jeopardy. They do this by showing us how to recognize and avoid sticky situations, thus averting the need to be defended altogether. In this manner, they educate us in the ways of the otherworlds so that we possess a greater awareness in our spiritual and magical work. Though our guardians walk with us always, they function as a helper, not a lifeguard. Once we have built a strong relationship with our guardian, just as a human big brother or sister might do, they can and will intervene on our behalf when we plop ourselves within reach of a dangerous situation. However, until we meet them, open to sense them, give them permission to work for us at full capacity and learn how to work with their signals, the relationship is only half of what it is meant to become.

As men and women of spirit interested in the pursuit of our spiritual and magical practices in this exceedingly complex and fast-paced world, tending the relationship with our guardian is nothing short of mandatory. Once we cultivate a strong and clear relationship with the guardian spiritual forces on our council, we are much better prepared to enter into the deeper zones of spiritual and magical work knowing we are taking seriously our task to remain safe, balanced and fully awake in our practices. Our first duty in cultivating this relationship to its utmost is to meet our guardian. Before speaking to this process, I would like to be sure we are all beginning this work from the same personally empowered foundation. This foundation requires us to scrutinize or vet all new inner contacts.

Vetting New Inner Contacts

When we set forth to explore any unseen ally be it an inner contact, a deity within our tradition, our guardian spiritual force, or members of our council, it is important to do so methodically and carefully. To set the foundation for this piece, I would like to speak to the practice of vetting the spiritual beings and energies associated with sacred sites and holy places in nature.

Many spiritual practitioners I know love to travel to ancient sites, spiritual power centers, cultural ruins and the like in hopes of sensing and communing with the spiritual forces that reside there. While these experiences can be wonderful, they can also be extremely unsettling and even harmful if embarked upon haphazardly. As stated in the Foundations and Definitions section of this book, the web of otherworldly energies is complex. Thus we cannot rely on the supposed purity of any particular natural place or physical space no matter how "holy" it is purported to be. All fields of force and form must be approached with caution if they are new to us. I cannot count the number of times friends and colleagues have relayed stories of their entering the most sacred site or holy place, only to find themselves unexpectedly zapped by an otherworldly negative/ retarding spiritual being or energy. We must remember that sacred places often inspire people to dump their emotions, sins and woes in an effort to cleanse or purify themselves. This is a natural human tendency and quite prevalent in churches, cathedrals, sacred sites and the like. If located in a compatibly vibrant and healthy natural setting, sacred sites can usually recycle the waves of human dumping that occur there. Many natural environments, however, are impaired by the human overlay which prevents them from functioning in a manner consistent with the natural destruction and regeneration process. So we cannot be sure, at first blush, how clean a natural site's field of working is until we investigate its inner terrain. If a sacred site is located within a typical four walled human built structure that is removed from the natural cycles of destruction and regeneration, human emotional releases typical to these places can aggregate. If persons trained to work with scavenger energies are not actively clearing these sacred places in a constantly vigilant manner, the residue left behind by human dumping can build and, over time, become increasingly unhealthy. The personal dumping/purification tendency just referenced explains why actual sacred sites are sometimes located near, but not at the point where the general population observes them to be. Frontage sites are often composed of the architecture and fanfare that serves as the human focal point where incidental dumping cannot quench the true spiritual energy which is housed a short distance away in an unmarked place. Very few places routinely employ scavenger-sensitive Priests and Priestesses who are trained to deal with energetic muck. Thus when we commune with the beings and energies permeating a sacred site we must not blithely open our deepest spiritual sensing at the start. We should instead, open stage by stage in discerning manner; I will describe one means of doing so as proposed by author and man of spirit, Frank MacEowen.

A few years ago I picked up Frank MacEowen's book *The Spiral of Memory and Belonging*. Tucked within the pages of this rather remarkable book is a reliable and practical means for entering into communion with otherworldly energies located in a place; Frank calls it *The Cycle of Multidimensional Awareness (The Cycle)*:

> *I find the image of a triangle with three different realms to which we can orient our consciousness helpful in grasping what I call multidimensional awareness. The first realm is simply that of ordinary reality...The second realm to which we turn our awareness is the energy of our own soul...The third domain is the realm of the Unseen, the parallel dimension of the spirit-energy that we can feel, that can influence ordinary reality, but that we cannot perceive with ordinary physical site.*[54] – Frank MacEowen

Upon reading his proposed method, I decided I would put his method to the test. I used *The Cycle* to carefully make contact with the otherworldly imprints in Jerusalem, the Galilee, the Occupied Territories near Bethlehem, Glastonbury, ancient sites in Southwest England, Pugent Sound, New York City, a Florida beach and my own beloved temple, The StarHouse. On each occasion, I was able to appropriately enter into, discern within and exit from my spiritual relationship with any natural place or physical space I encountered. Though no secondary recanting matches an author's original rhetoric, I will briefly describe the physical space and natural place "vetting" process of *The Cycle* below based upon my own experience in using it. I, of course, encourage readers to acquire the original resource as well.

The first phase of *The Cycle* focuses on our dense physical sensing abilities. In this phase use your eyes, hands, ears and feet to observe and acclimate to all the physical aspects of the natural place or physical space you are encountering. This observation and acclimatization should encompass all of the data our physical body can grasp including color, texture, signs, plant life, light, material information, smells, people, temperature, symbols, sounds, etc. This aspect of *The Cycle* grants our mind and body the means to acquire the physical data that allows our denser aspects to become familiarized. Familiarization of this nature puts both the brain and nervous system in a place of quieter receptivity. Because a mind and nervous system at rest can pick up the clear signaling of the unseen world in a much more

---

[54] MacEowen, Frank. *The Spiral of Memory and Belonging: A Celtic Path of Soul and Kinship*, New World Library, Novato California, 2004.

reliable manner, this first step is an important one. From here we open what Frank calls our "energy-body" and I would call our vital body to observe what we sense or feel when we are in relationship to the place or space. Phase two relies upon the same subtle sensing mechanisms of the physical body system we have been cultivating throughout this book. As such, it is the phase within which our guardian is most likely to offer its feedback. Through this second extension of our physical senses we will receive signals and impressions which inform us whether or not to proceed further. If upon opening to the subtle forces of our vital body we feel drained, sore, tired or anxious we should assume our allies are signaling a "no" to our further exploration. If instead we feel warm, open, light, full and spacious we may assume our allies are signaling a "yes" to the same inquiry. If we feel we have received a "yes" to continue, we move into the third phase of *The Cycle* by extending our senses further outward to receive the spiritual beings and energies of the place or space. At this point our strongest means of extended or intuitive sensing (e.g. sight, hearing, feeling and knowing) will guide us. Though Frank does not mention this in his book, when I exit my relationship with a place or space I find it helpful to work *The Cycle* backward. Aware of my spiritually extended senses, I pull them backward into my vital body and from here back again into a full appreciation of my physical body. I find this retraction helps me integrate the experience as well as assure my ability to move on from the moment intact and competent to drive, walk or speak to another person.

The Cycle assists us in vetting the spiritual integrity of physical spaces and natural places. What about vetting beings and energies we encounter in the inner realms through meditation or ritual? When we vet the spiritual beings and energies we encounter in our spiritual and magical practices, we utilize the same principles references in *The Cycle*, but we do so in a slightly different manner. Just as many of us would like to think every sacred site is void of any malice or ill will, many of us like to believe that any being or energy we call forth from the unseen worlds is benevolent in its intent. Through the course of this book, you have already learned that benevolence and love cannot be assumed in all otherworldly contacts. Thus it is important not to take any new spiritual contacts at face value. Just as we would cautiously and methodically assess our compatibility with the particular spiritual energies and beings within a place or space, when presented with any new spiritual contact through meditation or ritual, we must assess them too.

Vetting a new spiritual contact is no different than interviewing a new housemate. Thus we should engage the new contact in a kind of "housemate" interview process that allow us to assess whether or not they are appropriate and well suited for us. When we inquire into the substance of new spiritual contacts, we are better able to discern their nature, capacity and measure of appropriateness. Though less likely to be an issue, we must remember to take into account both the physical location and spiritual occasion when we meet with a new inner contact. If, for instance, you are doing a ceremony in the middle of a seventeenth century battlefield, you should use more caution than would be required if you are meditating in a well-attuned temple with a reliable spiritual teacher.

When coming to you through meditation or ritual, you will likely already be in a working containment with a dedicated candle lit. From here, you simply put the new inner contact "on hold" while you proceed through the steps in this vetting process. If you are not in a working containment, cast a sacred sphere around yourself. From here speak aloud or clearly think (if the occasion does not permit you to speak aloud) your *Central Flame* statement. Next, call upon the Name or Oversoul in whose honor your *Central Flame* burns. These are both important steps for they declare and define you in the inner worlds. Once you have done these two things, orient to the sensing and thinking capacities of your physical body system in response to the presence of this new spiritual contact. If you feel a "green light" response from your subtle body, you may proceed to extend your senses further into the spiritual dimensions. Once here, other aspects of the new contact will open out which may affect your inner sight, hearing or senses. At this point, ask these two questions: "What is your purpose in coming to me now?" and "What spiritual force(s) works through you?" Record the answers to this inquiry. If you are satisfied with the new inner contact's answers to the questions, you may engage with them at this time or in the future. If you are not, they will likely know this and vanish without any prompting from you; however, if they do not, simply tell them you are not willing to accept their offer of connection at this time and cut their connection to your sacred imagination.

These two vetting questions will tend to part the veils that open you to greater information, enabling you to discern this new contact's true nature and spiritual orientation. Would you do anything less to a stranger presenting themselves at the door in answer to your advertisement for a housemate? Of course not. As has been said before in this text, most often our other-worldly work corresponds directly to similar situations in the physical world. Thus, we must consider our unseen ventures and alliances just as carefully and methodically as we would consider the ventures and alliances of the physical world.

Remember this always: we do not have to say "yes" to every spiritual opportunity presented to us as if the unseen worlds are perfect and without flaws. As previously stated, we work with a council of unseen forces; within its influence and our other human/spirit co-creative webs there are certain elements that are chosen for us and certain elements we must choose for ourselves. If you are uncertain which inner contacts are appropriate for you, it is best to rely on the instruction of persons who have journeyed a bit further down your particular spiritual path to assist you in this matter. If you read books or take courses created by well known and well founded spiritual teachers, they will often offer meditations that introduce you to appropriate, reliable inner contacts within the unseen worlds. Inner contacts such as these have proven themselves to be steadfast in assisting men and women of spirit in their spiritual and magical work. Once you build a strong alliance with the well established inner contacts within your particular spiritual tradition, they will also assist you to assess the efficacy of any newer inner contact's intention and purpose. With our responsibility to vet all new contacts in mind, let us discuss the means by which we can each meet the guardian spiritual force that works within our council and/or chosen spiritual orientations.

Meeting and Relating to Your Guardian

In the previous section, I mentioned the importance of developing a reliable relationship with our guardian. I also mentioned that this relationship relies largely upon the meditative practices that will enable us to learn both their subtle communications and their teachings which help us to avoid otherworldly perils. To develop a sense of presence between us and our guardians, we must first directly and purposefully call them forth. In an effort to assist in this manner, the following introductory meditation and practical information is offered.

Meditation to Meet the Guardian

Find at least one hour when you can work at your altar undisturbed. In the usual manner, center yourself in the stillness of your own quieted being for a minute or two by gradually letting go of your attunement to prior occupations. Light a dedicated candle flame. Acknowledge the directions in creating the sacred sphere surrounding your field of working. Finally, speak aloud your Central Flame statement. In this sacred containment speak your intention to meet your guardian spiritual force. Something like, "I ask to meet the guardian spiritual force that will help defend and educate me with regard to the mysteries of the adjacent worlds I encounter" will suffice. From here, extend your subtle sensing abilities and wait in silence for a response from the appropriate otherworldly contact. Within the span of thirty seconds to a minute, you should feel the approach of a somewhat dense being or energy that appears to envelope or surround you in a protective fashion. Once you notice the form and force of this being, take caution to register its feeling very carefully.

If you do not sense this presence within one to two minutes, then trust that today is not the day for you to perform this task. Back out of the meditation by retracting your extended senses and come back into stillness. Wait a few days for more amiable aspects and resume this working again. Re-read the Prayer of the Priest and Priestess that is offered at the beginning of this book and trust that the time will soon come for you to complete this work.

If your guardian does present itself to you at your first sitting, remember to ask the two vetting questions referenced in the preceding section. Do not hesitate to be thorough. All new inner contacts should be questioned until you are satisfied with the results; only malevolent spirits become restless upon meeting our lines of questioning. Once you have thoroughly inquired as to the appropriateness and nature of this new inner contact, you may open fully to the presence of your guardian by asking it how it will work with you. To do this, extend all of your senses into the sphere of its influence so that you find a way to see, sense, hear, smell and know its presence. Be specific and take your time. Spend at least fifteen minutes in this many layered, full body experience so that your physical body system can both acquire this new data and recognize it again in the future. Be sure to include questions which will clarify the way your guardian will alert you to the presence of any negative/retarding spiri-

tual beings or energies you encounter. When you have completed the data-gathering aspect of this initial meet and greet meditation, thank this being for its service and ask if it needs anything else from you to strengthen your alliance. When you have received any information needed in this regard, release the connection, release your field of containment and sit in stillness for another minute or so to integrate this new information physically. Next, make notes in your journal pertaining to this initial experience of your guardian and what you need to remember in working effectively with it. Make a note to your-self that you will return to this communion within three days to begin the educational aspects of this new relationship.

As committed, three days later, follow the same progression you did before: stillness, create a field of working, speak your in-tention (this time it shifts from meeting to learning how to work safely within adjacent worlds), light your candle and speak your *Central Flame* statement. From here your guardian is in charge. It will offer you the instruction you need in the sequence that best fits your abilities and aspirations. Your guardian will also instruct you how often you should return for additional educational sessions.

In working with our guardians we must remember two prin-ciples from the Foundations and Definitions section. The work of developing a spiritual discernment practice is ours; a teacher can only point to the trail head, the journey up the mountain is our own. So while I can offer information as to the existence of guardians and how to begin to work with them, you must carry on from here. Secondly, we must be clear of fantasy and illusionary tendencies to accurately work with the spirits and beings of the unseen worlds. If you are not keeping up with your own process of releasing old unlawful images and staving off new unlawful images, illusion may pepper your work with a guardian.

Before completing this section on meeting our guardians, I would like to speak about their relative rank within the unseen worlds so that you are well acclimated to their otherworldly ori-entation. Take a moment to refer again to the figure entitled *A Sampling of Otherworld Relationships* presented on page 13; as you do, note where guardian spiritual forces lie within the relative ranking of otherworldly hosts. There you will see that guard-ians are placed somewhere in the middle of the stratum of oth-erworldly beings. Why is this so? Guardians are the day-to-day protectors/teachers that instruct us and help defend us from malevolent beings and energies. They function somewhat akin the role that the popularized term "guardian angel" describes; however they are not exactly this and we should not think of these beings in the same somewhat youthful manner. Guardians usually consist of either a specialized spirit being within of our council or a particular expression of our Higher Self. There is no "one-size-fits-all" spiritual description of a guardian as they vary slightly from person to person. However, there are common attributes that all guardians hold and functions that they perform. Let us spend a few moments speaking to these attributes and functions.

By and large, guardians do not consist of the exalted or higher ranking angelic or Archangelic forces. As mentioned before, all beings and energies function well within their own particular bandwidth but not so well beyond it. Before you sigh in despair, it is important to realize that the relative placement of our guardians is by design. Although the Archangelic forces summonsed amass would perhaps be most effective in protecting us from most all malevolent forms and forces, they are not naturally oriented toward individuals. Instead, Archangelic forces are oriented toward the whole of humanity and planet Earth. As such, they have specific tasks to perform and are not fixed to the physical body system of any particular human being as a guardian can be. Our alignment with the Archangelic forces will be addressed further on when our discussion steers away from the day-to-day and toward specialized situations. In contrast, lower-level guardian spiritual forces are individually dedicated. In addition, their placement makes them much better acclimated to the density of the physical world and all its complex circuitry. To be sure, both the particular personal and physical orientations of guardians are quite advantageous to those of us living within the human form. Their relative proximity to the physical world and to humans in particular, enables them to impress upon our physical body system in rather overt ways. As you work with your guardian you will undoubtedly find yourself grateful of their relatively dense nature and physical approximation.

To be clear, it may be helpful to explain the difference between a guardian and higher spiritual forces using an academic system as our comparative model. In college, entry level classes are often taught by a graduate assistant (e.g. guardian). In pursuit of his or her own advanced degree, the graduate assistant knows all of the basics and can effectively impart entry level information to the class of undergraduates. And, the graduate student is readily available on a day-to-day basis for a smaller allotment in the number of students he or she instructs. The tenured professor (e.g. higher level spiritual force) who holds a position of ultimate knowledge and authority, and is employed by the University (e.g. highest orders of Universal beings and energies) as the accountable entity, steps in to instruct the class once per week. The professor imparts his or her extensive knowledge in these less frequent sessions and then ventures back into the world of their own specialized pursuits which makes them the academic assets that they are. The interaction between us, guardians and higher level spiritual forces functions similarly to the interaction between a student, graduate assistant and tenured professor.

Ways in Which Guardian Spiritual Forces Intervene

Now that an understanding of the relative rank and position of guardian spiritual forces is understood, it may be helpful to learn how these beings tend to alert us to the perils of the otherworldly beings and energies. To illustrate how we may expect a guardian to assist us, I will relay an example from my own work. One evening as I slept in an old hotel located within a foreign country I was visiting, I was awakened by the physical sensation that something was pressing up against my body. I felt I was being sandwiched between two great pads or wings that were pressing against my skin in a pumping manner. In a semi-drowsy, just awakened state, I lazily asked myself what was going on. The familiar presence and voice of my guardian made itself known to me. Through imagery planted in my sacred imagination, my guardian showed me that a dangerous otherworldly being was trying to breach the boundaries of my physical body system. To thwart the invasion, my guardian wrapped itself around my body. It told me to lie still and be calm while it parted a veil and let me see what was happening in the hotel room. I saw several partially formed entities hovering above my and my fellow traveler's bodies in a manner similar to that of a swarm of mosquitoes. With this educational view in my consciousness, my guardian whisked me into a white and gold holding chamber where I was allowed to return to sleep for the duration of the night. When I awoke at dawn, I was a little tired, but otherwise fine. Unfortunately, the rest of my party woke physically sick and exhausted from the draining effect of the parasitic entities we had encountered.

The events of my eve in the haunted hotel are a relatively dramatic example of the kind of assistance one can expect from a guardian. When we stay in bed and breakfasts, hotels and hostels we will often encounter an imprint left by a previous resident of the hotel room or the land upon which the building was built. All kinds of unusual activities occur in hotel rooms; we will benefit from remembering this as we travel to and fro. Many people are impervious to these imprints, which is good for them. I used to be more resistant to parasitic beings and energies; however, I have found that the more spiritual work I do the more sensitive I have become to disturbed fields of energy. For some this is simply a consequence of deeper spiritual work. Recall from before, when our sensitivities increase to the subtle impressions of the benevolent spiritual beings and energies of unseen worlds, they also increase to those of the malevolent. When, due to one of the aforementioned circumstances, particular transient energies or place-based imprints present themselves we are likely to be drawn into the field of influence of the being or energy present, at least initially. Again, our guardian is able to watch over and alert us to the presence of these disturbances. From here it is up to us to respond appropriately. In a further section on physical-spiritual hygiene, I will discuss some of the ways in which we can cleanse and attune sleeping and living spaces. If you travel a fair amount as I do, when you read that section take note of the cleansing agents you feel you can pack into your suitcase to remediate unhealthy imprints in your travel accommodations. Once your guardian arouses you in a hotel setting, rise and put these tools into action before your physical body system bears the impact. As you work with your guardian you will learn the particular way it communicates the warning signs of parasitic activity to your physical body system. In addition to being unique to both you and your guardian, the signs and signals you receive from them will also vary depending upon your state of consciousness, specifically whether you are asleep or awake.

To begin, let us explore the signs and signals one can expect when encountering a negative/retarding spiritual being or energy during sleep. Contrary to the hotel example I just mentioned, not all negative/retarding spiritual beings and energies are encountered away from home. Even if we keep our homes well attuned, particular cosmic (e.g., particular solar or lunar alignments), ambient (e.g., weather patterns) and external conditions (e.g., local carnivals, street fairs and the like) can produce a transient spiritual imprint that wafts through our homes on occasion. Because we are typically relaxed in our homes, we can miss the subtle changes that indicate the presence of transient beings and energies that may drift through. However, when sleeping the imprint made by such beings and energies usually becomes more pronounced. During sleep transient beings will invade our physical body system for sustenance and impart the usual survival or sensual dreamscapes that keep us locked in sleep as previously described. Whether home or away, when we encounter parasitic energies and beings during our sleep, our guardian will alert us to the situation. Usually these alerts come in the form of a gentle jarring of the physical body in such a way that we are made aware of the invasion. Most people experience these alerts in the form of a light electrical shock to a body zone, a bell tone in the inner ear or a bright light kindled within our inner eye. In extreme situations we may feel additional firmness associated with our guardian's alerting and protecting activities such as the full body padding I described feeling in the haunted hotel. In all cases, whether offered gently or with firmness, it is our job to respond to our guardian's alert signals accordingly. Feeling tired and drained from the interruption of sleep's restoration, one may be inclined to ignore their guardian's signals in an effort to secure our rest, which of course continues the drain on our system. If we do not respond to their signals, our guardians cannot assist us. Again, they are here to help protect us; we must fulfill our part of the bargain by responding promptly and appropriately.

Appreciably, building spiritual discernment muscles during sleep is a trickier business than building them while awake. First, during sleep we are not fully conscious of the physical world thus our mind is not as physically perceptive as it is when we are awake. Second, dreams can be very difficult to interpret. How do we know the difference between an unhealthy dream induced by a parasitic entity and an unhealthy dream induced by our own inner psychological landscape? The frank answer is sometimes we don't. However, most of the time we can assess the quality of the dream and thus determine whether or not it is indicative of our need to do our own inner work or the unhealthy imposition of an external being or energy. If you encounter sleep interruptions or strange dreams and are not sure whether the interruption is your psychologically illuminating friend or spiritually debilitating foe, consider the quality and atmosphere of the interruption or dream. In all cases when I experience psychological dreams, the quality and content feels very personal and usually relates to something I am going through during my waking life. When I am in the midst of a parasitically induced dreamscape it feels very different and quite foreign. Often in these situations, my personal interactive abilities elude me. For instance, I may not be able to speak in the dream or my body will feel confined. I have come to learn that these particular dream occurrences signal the presence of a parasitic entity. Further, a guardian will interrupt externally-impressed sleep cycle disturbances. However, they normally do not interrupt a personal, psychological sleep cycle disturbances. By and large, guardians interrupt unhealthy sleep cycles by sending a signal to our physical body system that alerts us the invasion, while parasitic beings interrupt healthy sleep by inducing a state of fear, discomfort or pain. Over time, you will come to know the difference between upsetting dreamscapes induced by unhealthy parasitic activity and upsetting dreamscapes produced by your own personal psychological processes.

When we are wide awake our guardians tend to work in a slightly different manner than they do when we are sleeping because more of our personal faculties are available at that time. In these instances we will often notice sudden feelings of irritation, discomfort, exhaustion, energetic pricks against our skin or a change in bodily temperature. In some cases, we will even receive a strong and direct inner message. Though the obvious challenges to sleep state alerts were mentioned previously, in other ways sleep states provide beneficial conditions for our guardian's intercession because our consciousness is often quite rigidly focused in our waking life. Once into the rhythm and routine of our day, some people's consciousness can become so focused on the physical tasks before them that they are less receptive to their guardian's messages than they are when sleeping. If you are a person who routinely pushes past thirst, hunger or a need for the restroom while hammering away at your personal computer for hours on end, you may represent this remark. An awakened state does not always constitute an alert and fully present state. Therefore, when we are awake and maneuvering through the course of our day, we must develop other faculties for receiving and interpreting our guardian's alert signals. These faculties consist of any means by which we can create space between our mental and physical occupation and our vital body. There are varying ways to do this such as taking frequent work breaks, breathing exercises to relax the physical body system, five minute meditations and practicing the shift from focused vision to peripheral vision. We can practice these space-gaining exercises while standing in line at the motor vehicle department, walking through our backyards or in our car waiting for a train to pass on the tracks before us. Once space is created within our waking physical and mental occupations, we will be better able to sense our guardian's alert signals. When such signals are detected, we must further discipline ourselves to stop whatever we are doing and open to our guardians in meditation for clarity and instruction. Once we receive the clarity we need, we can address the situation in whatever manner is most appropriate.

Working with my guardian for some time now, I have learned that while there are negative/retarding beings and energies that it can readily thwart, there are others against which its particular abilities are less effective. However, through meditation I have learned how to more clearly detect and avoid the beings and energies my guardian is less able to help me with directly. It goes without saying that before working well together, I had to make time to open myself to my guardian's communication style and the teachings it imparts; you will need to do the same. Developing a relationship with an inner contact like a guardian takes time. Though the meeting meditation offered earlier in this section will provide an immediate connection, a tried and true working relationship with a guardian does not happen overnight. If we hope to be able to rely upon our guardian when we need them, we must spend time working with them when we don't. The same is true of all safety procedures. Remember the fire and tornado drills we endured in school? Going through the motions of the drill when not in a position of immediate need built a form in our minds that we could immediately call up when and if our school was threatened. This is one of the reasons why a daily spiritual practice is so essential for men and women of spirit. Repeated practices build spiritual muscles that come immediately into action when needed. Without them, you may find yourself in a time of need with little knowledge of what to do or how to proceed.

Working with the Beings and Energies of the Higher Realms

The Archangelic forces are perhaps the most exalted spiritual beings with which the majority of humanity is currently capable of working. As such, it is wise to consider developing a relationship with them as part of your personal spiritual practices. Though our day-to-day needs do not normally require their higher capacities, if we engage in our spiritual and magical work long enough, at some point we will likely find an occasion to require their assistance. If we build a strong relationship to the Archangelic forces when we do not need their intervention, we can call upon the strength of this relationship when, and if, we do. Beyond our own personal needs, it is appropriate to cultivate a relationship with the Archangelic forces because they play such an important part in the care and evolution of the planet and all its life forms. A relationship with these forces will enable us to accurately tune into the Earth's creative currents and offer our own prayers toward its healing. We must remember, rarely is it all about us, our lives and our trials and tribulations. As men and women of spirit we are here to serve the greater good. When we have elevated and deepened our consciousness such that we can tune into and commune with the Archangelic forces we are better able to serve this greater good from a place of selfless devotion and transpersonal focus.

Whether for personal aid or to better assist the greater good, our spiritual and magical work may take us into a field of resonance where the capacities of these more exalted spiritual forces are needed. Recalling the previous academic analogy, when we perform personal rites of passage, attend a birth or death, offer our ritual or meditative energies toward the healing of war or famine or engage in a spiritual dialog with folk souls and ancestral imprints, we may find ourselves beyond the capacity of the graduate assistance and in need of the professor. In these instances the Archangelic forces are appropriate and effective otherworldly allies. Before we can reliably work with these powerful spiritual forces, we must again build the spiritual muscle that creates the steadfast connection to them. This can be achieved through meditation, visualization and specific ritual workings. As is always the case, before opening to any new spiritual force it is important to define the parameters.

There are varying sources of esoteric wisdom available to us that describe the powers and abilities of the seven Archangelic forces. Though there are some differences and distinctions among these various sources, it is generally understood that the Archangelic forces are not human-featured angels carrying various tools representing their power and purpose. Instead, the Archangelic forces are an amassment of kindred spiritual and cosmic energies that embody unique and particular power, purpose and form in service to the planet earth and the greater cosmos. If one thinks of the force with which a swarm of bees directs itself through the air in sacred geometrical form, you are closer to an accurate description of these beings. Each Archangelic force is an embodiment of a principle of creation and as such is available to humanity and the Earth as a guiding spiritual force. The following poem written by W. G. Gray in his book *Exorcising the Tree of Evil* is not only elegant and beautiful, it is a helpful means of understanding the capacities and distinctions among the Archangelic forces:

*First we must accept there is good **Guidance** from on high,*
Then we have to seek a **Fount** *of spiritual supply,*
*When we get these connected by a line of **Truthful Light**,*
The other four are almost bound to come exactly right.

***Alertness** is essential for all action to commence,*
***Uprightness** proves the standpoint we should take up in defense.*
***Compassion** is the antidote to venomous intent,*
***Caution** must be always used unto its full extent.*

If anyone would change a state of Hell into a Heaven,
They could take great advantage of this Spiritual Seven,
And something far too obvious to classify as rumour,
A faculty that once was called an honest sense of humor.[55]

– W. G. Gray

Woven within this poem are references to the seven Archangelic Forces: *guidance* represents the crown and divine know-

---

[55] Gray, William G. *Exorcising the Tree of Evil*. Kima Global Publishers, Cape Town South Africa, 2002, p. 194.

ing of Metatron; the *fount* represents the cube of the Earth and the directed provisions of Sandalaphon; *truthful light* represents the cord and confident knowing of Suvuviel; *alertness* represents the sword and mental preparedness of Raphael, *uprightness* represents the lance and conviction of Michael, *compassion* represents the cup and mercy of Gabriel and *caution* represents the shield and common sense of Uriel[56]. To help familiarize yourself with these beings and provide a means of deeper meditative experience, keep a copy by your altar. I have found that its recitation prior to my meditation strengthens my reception to and knowing of the Archangelic forces.

When called, the Archangelic forces act as a filter of spiritual discernment between our physical body system, the physical world and the adjacent worlds. When we appeal to the Archangelic forces for their assistance it is best to imagine ourselves surrounded by or encompassed within a field or body of energy versus visited by a single caricaturized being. Though these beings are very powerful, we must be mindful of our own responsibilities when we engage them for we can unwittingly decrease their effectiveness. First, though this is not always the case, for the most part we must call to the Archangelic forces as they are generally not self-initiating. Though there may be times in our life when higher spiritual forces assert themselves on our behalf, again these times are usually rare. Most of the time we must call to the higher spiritual forces when we find ourselves in need of them for they respect our free will to choose our own path and particular experiences. Second, to be effective in working with the Archangelic forces, we must permit our physical body system's natural sense extending abilities to go out to meet them. This means we open to their presence in a real and visceral manner as opposed to an intellectual or fantasized manner. Though most of our spiritual discernment work will likely center on the relationship between ourselves and our guardian, we should periodically set aside time to cultivate a reliable relationship with the Archangelic forces as well.

When beginning to build our relationship with the Archangelic forces it is appropriate to focus on the four forces that enable and empower the creative powers of planet Earth, they are: Raphael in the East mediating to Earth the spiritual power

---

[56] Ibid. p. 188-191.

of Life, Michael in the South mediating to Earth the spiritual power of Light, Gabriel in the West mediating to Earth the spiritual power of Love and Uriel in the North mediating to Earth the spiritual power of Cosmic Law. The simple form of meditation presented next can be useful in this pursuit. At the onset, you will need a compass, a shield or metal/wooden plate, a sword, a lance and a chalice. Please note, after the initial working, the shield, sword, lance and cup will become dedicated items and should not be used again in a mundane or alternative manner. Further, if these items have been used previously, they will have to be cleared of prior intent and rededicated to this one. The compass you will certainly need in physical form, however if you do not have the other four items do not despair and do not go out and spend a hundred dollars buying them. Instead, draw each item as beautifully and reverently as you can upon four separate pieces of paper. In and of itself, this exercise imparts a deeper connection to the Archangelic forces than that which stems from commercially acquired ritual objects. Alternately, you may also decorate four squares of crafter's felt for easier storage and longer term use. To do this, use scissors and fabric glue, cut out colorful representations of the shield, sword, lance and chalice and paste or sew them upon four felt squares colored black/brown, yellow/white, red/gold and blue/green respectively.

Archangelic Forces Meditation

Once you have acquired your shield, sword, lance and chalice in whatever manner you choose, find at least twenty minutes when you can be alone and undisturbed for meditation. Either indoors or in nature, create a circle upon the floor or the ground such that there is space to lie down inside it. Using your compass, determine the alignment of the four directions that are East, South, West and North. Place your items or pictures in each of the four directions. Set the compass aside and sit in the center of the circle facing any direction you choose. Shift your mind and body into a meditative stillness. Now, determine the direction and Archangelic force that will serve as your starting place. Though there is no rule of thumb, most people tend to start this meditation in the direction that feels most familiar to them. Again in the Western Esoteric Tradition, Archangel Uriel mediates the spiritual powers of the North and Cosmic Law, Archangel Raphael mediates the spiritual powers of the East and Life, Archangel Michael mediates the spiritual powers of the South and Light and Archangel Gabriel mediates the spiritual powers of the West and Love. Once you have made your choice, lie down with your head pointing directly toward the direction and corresponding force of your choice. Speak a simple prayer of intention, for example, "With sincerity of mind, heart and purpose I seek to commune with the Archangelic force that is Michael who mediates the spiritual powers of the South and Light." From here, while lying still energetically seal the soles of your feet and gradually open the crown of your head. Then open your meditative consciousness to invite the Archangelic force that is Michael, South and Light. Commune quietly with this Archangelic force for approximately 10 minutes, taking notice of all that occurs. When you are done, speak a prayer of release and gratitude, for example, "I release and give thanks to the Archangelic force that is Michael, South and Light...I bid you go in peace." Still lying down, open the soles of your feet and allow any accumulated energy to flow into the Earth as a blessing. Close your crown, seal the soles of your feet and sit up again in the center of the circle facing any direction you choose. Reorient your mind and body to the whole of the physical world that exists all about you and return to your waking consciousness. Pick up your pictures or items and place them in a special box or on an altar where they can remain until you perform this meditation again. Make any notes you feel called to record in your journal to close the working. In a day or so, perform the meditation again choosing a different Archangelic force with which to commune. This simple meditation can be performed over and over again throughout your life for each time it is done, new and different experiences will offer themselves to you. In our spiritual and magical work in general, the benefit of repetition cannot be overstated. Repeating this meditation with the Archangelic forces will build the strong spiritual muscles that allow you to quickly and precisely call upon the exalted beings when you are in need of their assistance.

Finally, when we do find ourselves in need of the power and protection of the Archangelic forces and call to them as our cultivated relationship permits, we must concurrently release all fear, choosing instead a sense of complete trust in these exalted forces. It will not work to seal a circle in the name of these higher spiritual beings if we allow a panic-stricken imagination to run riot, picturing every conceivable kind of feared malice. When we vocally call upon the higher spiritual forces while physically and emotionally quaking in our boots, we are not truly open to their assistance. Fear closes certain portals of the physical body system that we need to have fully open to make the right decisions and take the right actions when we find ourselves in times of spiritual crisis. Just as we distinguished the word assessment which strengthens, from the word judgment that weakens us, we can distinguish words fear and respect which hold the same spiritual distinctions. If we allow ourselves to repel from the heights of invocation downward into the bowels of fear we will loose the power and ability to shift the current situation. Here is a brief example.

During one night's dreaming in the middle of an intense workshop focused on healing separation, I encountered the most gruesome folk soul I have experienced in my years working between the worlds. For what seemed like hours, I was thrown from one horrific and threatening scene to another all with the intent of frightening me and draining any ability I had to focus on the next day's workshop. At one point in the night having finally collected my wits, I stood upright in the black dream environment and shouted the names of the four Archangelic forces while declaring my alignment with them. At precisely that moment, I was boldly spat out from the dream's entrapment and back into waking consciousness. When I was able to come to my senses within the dream and thus remember and claim my true orientation, everything shifted immediately.

Remember that which occurs inside the unseen portals of our minds does not stay there. Our thoughts always magnetize like frequencies. If we wish to stand firm, clear and just in our spiritual and magical practices, then we must stand firm, clear and just in our innermost realms as well. To work successfully between the worlds, men and women of spirit must develop an ability to recognize and shift our reactions to otherworldly malice from a place of fear and overwhelm toward a place of assuredness and trust. Only from the place of assurance and trust can we loosen the grip of malicious otherworldly beings and energies and garner the full force and effect of the exalted spiritual forces. When we direct our consciousness to this place of orientation, we are better able to simultaneously attune to the working, prayer or meditation in which we are engaged and the guidance of the spiritual forces that work alongside us. In this way we can be alerted to any change of course that impacts the effectiveness of our spiritual work while also keeping ourselves spiritually and physically safe.

Developing and Maintaining a
Practice of Physical-Spiritual Hygiene

Thus far the focus of the Methods and Applications section has centered upon the importance of attending to the metaphysical aspects of spiritual discernment. At this point, it is appropriate to turn our attention toward attending the physical aspects of the same. In doing so, we venture into the fourth aspect of a spiritual discernment practice. Recall the PCA axiom mentioned in the context of taking caution not to get out of our depth: *"As above, so below...as within, so without."* This wisdom emphasizes the direct and reflective relationship between our inner and outer expressions. In the preceding section, the importance of this principle was underscored with reference to our inner thoughts and outer magnetizations. The same principle applies to other related aspects of our lives; specifically, the link between our spiritual and physical self. To maintain a reliable practice of spiritual discernment we must attend to the physical as well as the metaphysical. This requires us to focus upon the well being of our physical body and our living and working spaces. Throughout the course of my work, I have encountered many people who aim to live spiritually advanced lives in a physically polluted body, environment or both. Because our personal and ambient physical conditions impact our consciousness, well being and personal field of influence, be assured they affect the spiritual quality of our life as well. If we do not take care of our physical and external realms we run the risk of tainting our inner realms, too.

To be blunt, a well tuned environment and physical body system is much more difficult for unhealthy beings and energies to permeate. A well tuned environment is one that is created to reflect a balance of beauty and functionality. Once created, it is maintained with love and attention by its caretakers who routinely purify and re-attune the space to the sacred energies of Heaven and Earth. A well tuned physical body is one within which modes of work and rest, mental and physical exertion, pleasure and restraint are woven together in balance. Because this territory can produce particular sensitivities among men and women of spirit, let us expand upon it briefly.

If properly acknowledged, our physical body system will guide us away from that which undermines our health and toward that which augments it. It is up to us to listen to and respect our body's needs versus willfully circumvent them. Because spiritual work can be quite physically and emotionally demanding, as men and women of spirit we must responsibly cultivate and maintain our own well being to the best of our ability. Though this manifestation varies from individual to individual, filling our bodies with junk foods, smoking tobacco, consuming copious amounts of alcohol or engaging in other vitality depleting acts are certainly to be avoided. Beyond that, it is important that we develop a personal sensitivity for that which vitalizes us versus that which devitalizes us. Each man and woman of spirit is unique, thus each must determine the specifics of the lifestyle that best supports their spiritual and magical work and stick to it. If you judiciously employ the "what vitalizes me versus devitalizes me" litmus test, you will go far in keeping yourself in a good and healthy state. We all know that when we are tired, stressed and under-nourished, we run the risk of becoming a host for infectious diseases. When our physical body system is operating at low vitality, we are more susceptible to the influence of diseases of a spiritual nature. Recall the earlier mention of the work of Paracelsus and W.E. Butler who both spoke to the long term physical effects of persistent elementary beings that work through invisible fields of form and force to affect our mind, emotions and eventually our physical health. These same invisible forms and forces accumulate among environmental items such as paint and other chemical agents, military relics or weaponry, broken equipment, mold or mildew and a pantry filled with expired foods. Over time, environments populated by these substances become quite depleted of vital energy. This depletion manifests as a low energy field in the space. Fields of this nature attract like energies and beings from the unseen worlds; which exacerbate the unhealthy environment initially created through neglect. Anything that depletes the life force of a space can, in turn, deplete the life force of its human and non-human occupants, making them more susceptible to the influence of negative/retarding beings and energies in general.

In attending to the harmony and vitality present in our physical bodies and environment and thus staving off negative/retarding beings and energies, we should perform routine physical and spatial purifications. Purification of this nature includes our physical body system through rites of sweating, fasting, bathing, emotional release and our living and working environments through rites of cleaning, organizing, clearing and attuning. Physical body and environmental purifications are a very important part of a spiritual discernment practice. In ancient times, Priests and Priestesses of all traditions knew the importance of tending the physical body system and living space as a means of staving off negative/retarding spiritual beings and energies. Due to a combination of spiritual ignorance and the busy pace of our modern times, we seem to have lost this art of daily life. The following segment outlines what I call the five "Rs" of purification: reflect, refer, release, reclaim and return[57]. Before going on, I wish to be exceedingly clear. Physical-spiritual hygiene does not in and of itself rid your physical body and environment of all negative/retarding energies and beings. It can, in some instances lift unhealthy imprints; however its mainstay is preventative. Purification rites keep your being and surroundings consciously clean of minor unhealthy energies. They also enable us to maintain a particular attunement between physical matter and spiritual force which staves off affinity-based otherworldly attractions to begin with. Physical/spatial harmony is but one aspect of *The Pentacle of Spiritual Discernment*, the four other aspects are equally important in maintaining our spiritual well being. If you are dealing with a more sophisticated unhealthy being or energy pattern, you may need to call upon the assistance of the higher spiritual forces or colleagues further down the path for all the reasons outlined in prior sections of this book. In augmenting our spiritual discernment practice by paying attention to the details of the physical matter of our lives, we are simply working to keep ourselves and our environments as inhospitable to unhealthy otherworldly beings and energies as possible.

Step One: Reflect. To begin we engage in the stage called "Reflect." Here we assess the quality of the energies or imprints we are intending to release so that we can discern the best purification agent and method to employ. Reflecting upon and listening to the subtle messages of your body or physical space before choosing your agent is an important component of effective purification. Many newly interested men and women of

---

[57] This section is taken from *The Art of Purification* written for The Path of the Ceremonial Arts, by A.J. Nutt, copyright 2004.

spirit simply grab a bag of white sage from their local New Age bookstore and begin cleansing their homes before stopping to listen to the space and consider whether sage is the best agent to break up the particular accumulated energy pattern. Purification is not a "one-size-fits-all" affair. Within the inherently organic nature of our bodies and physical spaces, nothing stays the same over time. When we couple this changing nature with the tides and turnings of the unseen worlds, we double the potential for fluctuation. Thus it is always best to first reflect upon your particular purification needs before diving into physical or spatial purification rites. Personally, I have found it helpful to compile a personal tool kit consisting of the purification agents that work well in the specific instances I've encountered. Most of the time my accumulated list of purification agents, their affinities and corresponding properties suits my needs. However, on occasion, a new situation presents itself and I realize I need something new or different to achieve my aim. On these occasions, I perform research and use my intuition to make or acquire a new purification agent or combination of agents for the purpose. In this manner I keep learning and building my purification resources. Taking the time to reflect upon each purification situation is important, for it entices us to develop a specific and appropriately reliable tool kit based upon our own personal knowledge and experience.

Step Two: Refer. Step Two involves determining to where the released matter or energy shall be "referred" once it has been lifted from the physical body or space. Many practitioners skip this step, assuming that the cleansed energy knows where to go. If the energy is drawn to a place where you do not desire it to take residence to begin with, does it seem wise to think that it will know where to go after it is released? In all cases, it is best to consciously refer released energy to a specific exit point. When doing so, direct the energy to a place where it can be reabsorbed and recycled by the natural destruction and regeneration processes of the primal world. When I bathe to cleanse my physical body, I refer the released matter to the drain and Earth for recycling. When I cleanse my home, I open a window to the outside and direct the cleansed energy out the window and into the natural regenerative processes. Though simple, this action will improve the effectiveness of each purification rite you perform.

Step Three: Release. Step Three is the performance of the purification rite itself. As you begin, call to your inner contacts. Next state your purification intention and the referral location out loud. Speak a prayer requesting you be granted rightful use of the natural power of your purification agent for sacred service. Working in harmony with the power of your agent and your unseen allies, follow your intuition and inner guidance to perform the rite of cleansing. When working to clear a physical space, it is often best to begin the rite at a central focal point for the space, such as a central altar or front door. From here, move around the space in a methodical manner until all aspects of it are covered. Some practitioners prefer to cleanse in a counter-sunwise direction and re-attune in a sunwise direction. Others prefer to do both the cleansing and re-attunement in a sunwise direction. Each practitioner must find the manner that best suits their own preferences without becoming rigidly attached to form void of clarity of purpose. Even if you find yourself preferring a particular movement pattern stay awake in your practice, for some day you may be presented with a situation where that which has always worked needs to be adjusted to fit the current circumstance. If you approach your rites in a manner that is rote, you may miss the signals which necessitate a deviation from the tried and true.

Step Four: Reclaim. Once cleansed, our physical body or environment sparkles with new potential. It is somewhat like a freshly tilled plot of garden soil. Staying with the metaphor, if you do not plant what you wish to grow there, other plants will take advantage of the space and haphazardly populate your plot. Thus once you have completed the purification rite, it is important to bless and rededicate your body or physical space. For the most part, I reclaim my physical body by reciting my *Central Flame* statement which re-attunes me to my purpose and my spirit allies. Likewise, in my living and working spaces I recite a *Central Flame* statement that attunes them to their highest resonance and capacity. Many practitioners re-attune their sacred spaces to the power and harmony of the four directions of East/Life, South/Light, West/Love and North/Cosmic Law. Others re-attune their cleansed spaces in honor of a particular personal deity, God or Goddess. There are many ways to reclaim our physical bodies and spaces once a purification rite is complete. The key is to choose your re-attunement and repopulate the physical being or space with clear and sacred intention.

Step Five: Return. Step Five involves the thankful return of the cleansing agent(s) to the Earth. I have found this to be another very important and often overlooked step in the purification process. The act of returning our ally to the Earth pays tribute to the cycle of life, death and rebirth. It also reaffirms our gratitude for the purifying gifts of the natural world. The only rule of thumb in returning is to be conscious of the agent, its condition and the most appropriate means of natural incorporation. For the most part, I compost the remains of my purification agents whenever possible. The exception to composting is the use of salt and salt infused water because salts in concentration can disrupt plant life. Thus when returning salt to the Earth I scatter it over rocks in small quantities away from growing plants.

With the five basic steps involved in a physical purification rite in place, I will offer a brief overview of the general categories of traditional purification agents for those who are less familiar with the various means and methods available.

Purifying with Botanicals

Botanicals have been used for centuries as effective purification agents in fresh, dried or infused form. In fresh form specific, individual herbs, plants and flowers are selected for their purifying properties. Next, they are bundled together in a bouquet and brushed across or thumped upon the person or object being purified. If you are familiar with film *Goddess Remembered*[58] by Donna Reed, you may remember the scene in which a Mexican grandmother is singing while tapping and brushing the body of another with a bundle of fresh herbs. In dried form, botanicals are most often burned on charcoal tablets as a smudge. In infused form, they are steeped in hot water, cold water, alcohol or glycerin which infuses the medium with the beneficial properties of the herbs. Botanicals in all forms can also be mixed with sea salt to create wonderful grounding and purifying preparations. As previously mentioned, the task for the practitioner is learning what botanical to use in which situation. Any standard magical methods text will list a plethora of plants and corresponding properties from which to choose; however, there is no substitute for doing and logging your own ritual experimentation and re-

---

[58] Goddess Remembered, video directed by Donna Reed, Well spring Media, Inc. 1999.

search. Though standard information certainly does apply, intuition and experience are important to cultivate as well. As you begin to work with botanicals you will find that each person or place responds differently to each particular plant. Likewise, each field of disturbed energy responds differently to each particular plant. It behooves each of us to first learn the basic properties of each botanical we intend to use. From here, we should augment this knowledge through our own application. Considering botanicals in general, you will undoubtedly find that depending on the situation white sage, palo santo, eucalyptus, hyssop, thyme, lavender and copal are primary among purification agents that cleanse or purify a person, place or thing. Alternately, sweet grass, cedar, frankincense, sandalwood, myrrh and rosemary are primary among purification agents that reclaim, attune or bless a person, place or thing. As the title will reveal, an excellent resource to acquire for this work is Mrs. M. Grieve's two volume set *A Modern Herbal: The Medicinal, Culinary, Cosmetic and Economic Properties, Cultivation and Folk-Lore of Herbs, Grasses, Fungi, Shrubs and Trees with Their Modern Scientific Uses*. The original books were published in 1931, however Dover Publication's 1981 reprint edition of these indexes are easily found in reputable herb shops and online bookstores.

Purifying with Water

> *Running water, we know, has peculiar electrical qualities, as witnessed by its effect on the divining-rod in the hands of a sensitive person. Whatever it may be that affects the diviner is probably the same thing that affects the occult attack.* [59]
>
> – Dion Fortune

Water is perhaps the purifying agent with the greatest history of use. It is the life blood of nearly all organic matter; it not only sustains vitality, it whisks away impurities, cleanses and restores. For this reason it has been used for centuries as a primary purification agent. Customary religious ceremonies such as christening, baptism and the mikveh rites all rely upon water as the medium of cleansing and transformation. Further, wa-

---

[59] Fortune, Dion. *Psychic Self-Defense*, Weiser Books, Boston, MA/York Beach, ME. 2001, pg 187.

ter's crystalline structure has proven capable of holding the energetic imprint of musical sounds and the spoken word. In the book *Messages from Water* [60], Dr. Masaru Emoto, a revolutionary Japanese researcher, studied and documented the effect various sounds, words and phrases had on the crystalline structure of water. Researchers working alongside Emoto observed the difference in the crystalline structure of a water molecule when positive words, phrases and sounds were offered in its midst versus negative words, phrases and sounds. When, for instance, the phrase "You fool!" was spoken over a single water sample, the crystalline structure of water became distorted and diffused. Even after the sample was frozen and reexamined, the distortion did not change. When the phrase "Thank you!" was spoken over another water sample, the beautiful, crystalline structure was retained. The same response pattern occurred when water was subjected to violent heavy metal music versus beautifully orchestrated classical music. If water absorbs sounds, phrases and words then it absorbs prayers. If we speak a prayer into the water we intend to use in a ritual purification, its crystalline structure will resonate with our sacred intention and thus enhance our work. In ritual settings such as a purification rite, water is normally infused with salt. Salt's crystalline structure can also become imprinted and empowered by the spoken word. Used together, water infused with salt and prayerful words acts as a powerful purification agent for both our physical body and our living and working spaces. We can bathe in salt infused waters to purify and reconfigure the energetic patterning of our physical body system. We can also make light salt water solutions that can be spritzed or sprinkled throughout a physical space clearing it of stubborn, lingering unhealthy imprints.

Purifying with Light

Light is an often over looked purification agent. There are three basic forms of light used to purify the physical realm: radiant light, iridescent light and colored light. Radiant light comes to us by way of the sun, the stars or a dedicated candle flame. These brilliant and stronger forms of light are effective in illuminating and releasing negative energy patterns

---

[60] Beyond Words Publishing. *Messages from Water*, Hillsboro Oregon 2004. Written by Dr. Masaru Emoto Translated by David Thayne, 2004.

embedded within physical spaces, including the human body. When left in its rays for a period of twenty-four to thirty-six hours, solar radiation is very effective in destroying harmful bacteria, microbes and negative energetic imprints upon articles of clothing and physical objects. Light rays that emanate from the star beings of the heavens are also powerful agents of physical-spiritual hygiene. Using *naked eye astronomy* [61] one can pull starlight directly through the eye and into the heart and physical body system. Realization of this effect gives a whole new dimension to the notion of star gazing. Finally dedicated candles cast beams of blessed light in churches, temples and upon our personal altars. When prayerfully and intentionally attuned with the particular spiritual qualities desired in the space or place, the living flame in the center of all life is joyfully reinforced.

Iridescent light is different from radiant light because its source is hidden and thus invisible to most of us. It is the glow that emanates from within the deep Earth, the beam of healing that we send to another who is suffering and the radiance cast forth from the benevolent beings and energies of adjacent worlds. Though some claim to see iridescent light directly, this form of light is usually felt as opposed to seen. We feel this light as energy in the form of heat, "pins and needles" or prickling sensations of various intensities. The subtle tone of iridescent light transforms both our environments and dense physical nature of our bodies. We summon iridescent light by praying for its grace and by entering into a meditative communion with the forms and forces from which it emanates. Though quieter in its apparent nature, iridescent light can be extremely beneficial to the physical realms. To work with this quality of light, we can engage in meditation activities that allow this light to leave its normal place of residence and permeate your physical body system.

To engage with the spiritual power of iridescent light simply center yourself in stillness, then create your sacred sphere and call to your inner contacts as usual. From here use your sacred imagination to envision the light that exists within the natural world, the center of the Earth, the auras of living creatures and

---

[61] Naked eye astronomy is taught by All Seasons Chalice's StarWisdom project which offers tools related to sidereal astrology and Anthroposophy to the public. For more information on naked eye astronomy or StarWisdom, go to www.starwisdom.org.

the like. Once envisioned, invite this light to permeate your physical body system through the etheric body. Often when these connections are made, your body will become noticeably hotter, affirming your communion with the iridescent light to which we've become connected. This light and its particular energetic quality will alter your physical body system, so be mindful of the duration of meditations such as these.

Colored light is a form of purification that many of us do not consider when we purify ourselves and our spaces. However, few agents are as effective as color in shifting our mood and physical well being or setting a feeling tone for our working and living environments. We all know that color is created when particular rays of the visible light spectrum are reflected off of an object and into our eye. Each color's reflection imparts a unique feeling or mood, which in turn has the capacity to affect physical matter. In his book *Knowledge of Higher Worlds and its Attainment*, Rudolph Steiner explains the effect of colored light upon the feeling and spiritual sensing capacity of an individual. According to Steiner, we not only have the ability to see color with our physical eyes, we can also "see" color through our spiritual perception. Our spiritual perception of a color is composed of the feelings that are experienced when we integrate a physical color impression. Working with the feeling tones color creates within us is one way Steiner encourages us to awaken and strengthen our spiritual senses. Because they are inherently linked, anything that affects our spiritual senses has the capacity to affect physical matter. Colored light is very effective in its ability to help our body change state via its effect on our emotion. When employing colored light purification personally or spatially, first determine the color that suits your purpose (based upon your own relationship, versus a "system"). Though some may argue with this assertion, I do not think it is helpful to limit our knowing of light to things like popularized chakra or mood colors as this creates an over intellectualized relationship to color. Due to personal spiritual and psychological associations, the color red will affect one person differently than another. Rather, as Steiner suggests, one should employ colored light by connecting its hue to our own feeling capacity for the color impression we desire.

Purifying with Incense & Essential Oils

Call it psychosomatic, but they (essential oils) make us feel better and feeling better can have a therapeutic influence on physical symptoms. So much physical illness is in fact, to some degree, stress related...and...oils work on the physical body in a variety of ways...oils are among the most potent anti-bacterial agents known to man...they can be used to balance the subtle energy flows in the body.[62] – Robert Tisserand

In this quotation offered by the grandfather of modern aromatherapy, Robert Tisserand speaks to the benefit of essential oils from a folk knowledge basis. In his book, *Aromatherapy: The Essential Beginning*[63], Dr. D. Gary Young puts forth a scientific basis for the therapeutic effects to which Robert Tisserand speaks. In his research, Dr. Young found that when the body is in crisis due to stress or illness, the measurable electrical frequency of the physical body (or life force) drops, typically below 58 mHz. The key to improving health is to increase the frequency or life force of the body so it can once again thrive. According to Dr. Young, essential oils range in frequency from 55 mHz to 320 mHz (the frequency of rose oil). Dr Young's research has shown that when a living organism in crises is administered a high frequency essential oil, the result is an increase in frequency for the body. This increase in frequency can shift the course of or stave off illness altogether. Because oils literally shift physical and emotional patterns in the body, they are certainly wonderful to incorporate into our purification rites. In physical spaces I have had great success diffusing essential oils in a simple glass disc and tea candle diffuser. In my sleeping space I tend to purify the space with lavender oil before retiring at night to create a soothing atmosphere. Aside from the quieting mental effects of lavender, I find I benefit from its antibacterial and antimicrobial effects as well, for most often our bodies surrender to a cold or flu virus during sleep. In the morning, I diffuse an oil with a higher vibration such as frankincense. Frankincense lifts the night energy and fills the room with solar fire.

---

[62] Tisserand, Robert. *The Art of Aromatherapy*, Healing Arts Press, Rochester, VT, 1977.

[63] Young, N.D., D. Gary. *Aromatherapy: The Essential Beginning*, Essential Press Publishing, Salt Lake City, UT, 1995.

Essential oils come in single substance preparations and powerful blends, some of which are made especially for purification. In selecting essential oils for your purification rites, it is important that you endeavor to use therapeutic grade oils as opposed to pure essential oils. Often the extraction processes of the latter rely upon the use of inexpensive solvents. Because there is no guarantee that these solvents are completely removed from the product upon bottling, they are less desirable for use in purification rites. Therapeutic grade oils rely on chemical free steam distillation in their extraction processes. Before selecting any single oil or oil blend it is important to research the specific properties of the oil and recommended physical uses. To begin, research the oils you intend to use, noting all cautions offered. Document the properties and uses of each of the oils you study in a separate journal or on index cards. When you need purification oils, you can simply refer to your documentation to make your selection. Though not an exhaustive list by any means (and one must do one's own research), I have found the following information about commonly used essential oils to be reliable. My sources include the previously mentioned books written by Dr. Young and Mrs. M. Grieve. When you read about the physical, medicinal and ceremonial uses of the oils listed below, take a moment to picture the plant or tree in your mind. Upon doing so, see if you can intuit the ways in which these particular botanicals affect the beings and energies in the unseen worlds as well as the microscopic beings and energies in the physical body.

Benzoin – the balsamic resin of a far eastern tree, from Sumatra and Siam, extracted from an incision made in a living tree. Benzoin possesses anti-septic qualities, for centuries it has been thought to drive away evil spirits.

Cedarwood – tree resin, preservative used in mummification and temple wood preservation, calms mucous membranes, sedates and eases anxiety and nervous tension.

Eucalyptus – oil of leaves of eucalyptus trees of many varieties. It is a stimulant with strong antiseptic and anti-parasitic properties. It is a powerful disinfectant which also purifies the blood.

Frankincense – obtained from the leafy boswellia thurifera tree, extracted from an incision made into the tree. Frankincense is a powerful stimulant with centuries of ceremonial and religious uses. It was a component of the coal-based eye makeup mixture used by Egyptian women.

179

Hyssop – a leafy herb native to southern Europe with a long history of use in the cleansing of holy places. It assists in the remediation of rheumatism and bruising, regulates blood pressure and sedates the nerves.

Lavender – a woody herb indigenous to the mountains in the western Mediterranean, yet cultivated widely. It sedates the nerves of the heart, activity of the brain and improves the workings of the stomach. It assists in the relieving of depression and anxiety and possesses anti-inflammatory and pain relieving abilities.

Lemon – oil from the rind of the lemon. It possesses diaphoretic, diuretic and astringent properties. It briskly clears energy, enhances the immune system and benefits the skin.

Myrrh – gum from the myrrh bush in northeastern Africa & Arabia. It has been used for centuries in religious and ceremonial practices as well as embalming. It possesses many astringent and healing qualities including stimulating and strengthening the pulmonary system and restoration of the soft tissues of the mouth.

Rosemary – oil of a woody herb that has been used for centuries to strengthen and clear the mind as well as enhance memory. The ancients used rosemary for ceremonial purposes in place of more expensive incense. It is an excellent stomachache remedy and nervous system stimulant.

Thyme – a woody garden herb indigenous to the mountains of Spain and other European counties. It possesses powerful antiseptic, antispasmodic and antimicrobial properties. It assists the body in releasing phlegm and restoring deep breathing capacity.

Purifying with Sound

The purifying agents discussed thus far are, for the most part, all materially based; here we turn to the ethereal quality of sound as our agent. There is so much for modern day humanity to learn and experience where the healing qualities and powers of sound waves and harmonic vibrations are concerned. From the mathematical theories of the ancients, to harmonics of modern day sound healers, to the simple pleasures of the soundscapes that makes each individual heart sing, music has the power to touch us deeply. Previously I mentioned the book, *Messages from Water*, within which scientists documented changes in the crystalline structure of water as it was exposed to sound in the form of heavy metal versus classical music. We know that the same research has been done with plants in earlier years. Plants flourish when bathed in the serenade of elegant classical music and dwindle under the influence of raucous contemporary music. Just as color, texture and shapes create an environment, sound creates an environmental; and again all environments have the capacity to impact our physical body system and thus our well being.

The quality of music and sound is known to change our emotional state of being instantaneously. Our emotional state alters our physical state. The same change of state can be imparted into our physical environments when sound is used to purify them. Historically, I have used three different means of sound purification: 1) tonal vibration from specially cast bells, chimes and bowls, 2) my own voice in the form of songs, chants and tones, and 3) recorded sacred choral and instrumental music. One of my favorite means of using sound to purify my physical body is toning and chanting while in the bath or shower because the reverberation heightens the effect. Starting at the base of my spine, I find a tone that correlates my skeletal system with its kindred qualities of Earth and North. I sit with that tone for about thirty seconds before moving to a tone that correlates my lungs with its kindred qualities of Air and East. I move on to a tone that correlates my body's heat and its kindred qualities of Fire and South and then conclude with a tone that correlates my bloodily fluids and its kindred qualities of Water and West. At the conclusion of this simple toning, I literally feel a revitalizing sense within my physical body. In a spatial context, I tend to use my own voice in chant to re-attuning my living and working spaces. On occasion, I will also use singing bowls or chimes to do the same. I tend to use recorded music as a means of retaining, versus setting, the re-attunement of my sacred spaces. For I feel that we should each give ourselves to the attunement of our sacred spaces and not simply put on a piece of recorded music to do the job for us. However, once attuned, recorded music is perfectly appropriate to use in a maintenance capacity. The most powerful musical pieces I have used in this capacity are the rich and beautiful tonal chants of David Hykes. I also favor the works of the early European composers such as the masses of Byrd and Palestrina or the chants of Hildegard von Bingen.

Purification Layering

There is one final aspect of ritual cleansing that I would like to mention; it is called purification layering. Purification layering is a multi-dimensional rite that involves the use of several purification agents in a sequence, layering of one agent on top of another. Purification layering grants us the ability to affect various forms of matter and energy within the same rite. For this reason, I have found it to be most beneficial for clearing physical bodies and environments. For example, I mentioned toning through the elemental systems of the body as a great means to use sound to purify. I also mentioned I do this while soaking in the bathtub. This is an example of purification layering for the body. To offer a broader spectrum of purification in a physical space, I will layer the uniquely different energetic qualities of botanicals, oils, light or sound in succession.

To begin a rite using purification layering, first reflect upon the situation and assess which different agents to employ. Gather the oils, herbs, lights or sounds that you have assessed you will need. Then one by one, engage each agent in a sequence that affects the space; layer by layer releasing the negative energy more and more thoroughly. In most instances, it is beneficial to employ the agents sequentially according to their tonal qualities. Like the movement inherent in a musical scale, begin with the lowest toned agent (e.g. salt water, palo santo or cedarwood), then move to a higher toned agent (sage or eucalyptus) and conclude with the highest toned agent (frankincense or human sound).

I will offer a progression I have used purification layering to energetically cleanse my home as an example of purification layering. I always begin by reflecting upon the needs of my home at the time. Seasonal issues impact the purification needed as does the level of activity that my home has recently sustained. For the sake of illustration, let's say I chose salt-water, sage and sound as my agents for this day. With my reflection complete and my agents chosen, I determine the means to redirect the cleared energy. From here, I pray for the wisdom and grace to work in harmony with the agents I am choosing. And then I begin the cleanse. I start the purification of my home at my fireplace mantle as this is the heart center of my home. Using a salt-water preparation, I begin by moving around my house, spritzing and sprinkling the space to breaking up and release any accumulated energies. While doing so, I recite my prayers of release and reclamation. Once this is complete, I journey sunwise around my home fanning sage smoke throughout the house from top to bottom, repeating my redirecting prayers as I go. After circling the home, I imagine increasing the length of my arms, hands and fingers to psychically sweep energy from the high places where my smudge fanning may not have reached; I redirect these energies as well. Lastly, I walk around again offering sacred sound in the form of chanting. When the releasing step is complete, I re-attune by diffusing a sacred oil while speaking *The Central Flame* statement for my home to invite the presence of benevolent angels into this space. To conclude, I refer any agents used into their proper natural recycling process.

Life and Times: Other Helpful Aspects to Consider

Having discussed the importance of a well tuned physical body system and environment, let us now turn our attention to the non-personal physical systems we encounter during the course of our lives. Whether through work, recreation or travel, we come into physical contact with various forms and forces every day. We work in shared offices and buildings, shop in grocery stores, exercise in crowded gyms, recreate at packed music concerts or local festivals and so on. In each of these instances we will encounter the energetic imprints of other persons, places and things. Indeed some of these external energetic imprints affect our physical body system positively offering increased vitality, joy and connection which is wonderful. Obviously we are not concerned with the physical and energetic encounters that positively impact us. Our concern lies with recognizing and negating the impact of the physical systems that negatively impact us. If not recognized and responded to in an appropriate manner, over time our daily encounters with unhealthy persons, places and things can agitate the physical body system, resulting in chronic physical and emotional disturbances. Though not always, often times sudden, unexplainable fatigue and irritation are emotional and physical reactions to the way in which the subtle body is being affected by the unseen beings and energies in a place. To reiterate a point made earlier, when negative/retarding beings linger in a place it is usually because 1) they rely on their undetected or background nature to conceal their energetic presence, 2) there is a consistent flow of vital energy upon which these beings can feed or 3) the people encountered are naïve to their presence and potential effects, often assigning the symptom to another more logical origin.

In this regard, negative/retarding spiritual beings and energies permeate our physical body system via our own affinities and/or unguarded countenance. What was discussed in some length in the previous section pertaining to spiritual disturbances and their causes applies here as well. In the course of our daily lives, we can and do occasionally pick up sticky remnants that linger upon other people, places or things. Some of us are sensitive enough to immediately feel the effect of parasitic energies and beings; others are not as sensitive. Working with a guardian will certainly enhance your sensitivity and increase your own personal wellness awareness on a day to day basis. However, when you return home from what felt like a sticky or unhealthy environment, it can be helpful to perform a personal purification rite to help release any lingering imprints you might have involuntarily picked up.

Protective Talismans

Beyond working with a guardian and purifying ourselves after visiting strange or foreign environments, there is another preventive measure that men and women of spirit can incorporate in their spiritual discernment practices: the creation and dedication of a personally protective talisman. Many religious and spiritual traditions incorporate the use of protective talismans. Often we see members of the Catholic Church wearing medals depicting the likeness of a patron Saint. Many indigenous people carry with them or wear protective herbs and animal vestiges. Often, Earth-based practitioners wear or carry specially charged crystals, runes or magical symbols. People of various traditions place protective talismans in their cars for safe travel. Talismans are a well known and widely accepted means of reinforcing our self awareness and protection when we venture into the world at large. As with any magical tool, before a talisman can possess the power to thwart negative/retarding spiritual beings or energies, it must be imbued with a truly derived and effective spiritual imprint. Though there are certainly exceptions, factory made talismans purchased from your local esoteric retail store rarely carry any true or effective spiritual power. This is due in part to the detrimental effects of mass production and in part to the lack of relationship between the maker and the bearer. Mass produced spiritual items can be imbued with protective powers if the bearer understands the principles governing physical talismans. The key to an effective talisman is relationship. For a talisman to be effective, the bearer has to cultivate and maintain a personal and spiritual relationship to and through it. Effective talismans possess an ability to resonate with and, in turn, reverberate the appropriate personal and spiritual associations of the bearer. They are energetically charged, by the bearer, with the spiritual alliances and thought-forms to which its protective powers are dedicated. In her book, *Glastonbury Avalon of the Heart*, Dion Fortune speaks to the specific quality of connection required to impart a spiritual ability into a physical object.

> *Unless we can share in the inner life of a symbol, its outer form will convey nothing to us. Unless we have made a voluntary sacrifice for pity's sake, we will learn little from meditation on the Cross...The consecrating words of the Priest make a cup into a Chalice, but it is only the consecrating consciousness of the communicant which can change the Chalice into the Graal.* [64] – Dion Fortune

Spiritual symbols and representations are only as powerful as the bearer's connection to their otherworldly counterparts. When we utilize sacred objects such as candles, altar items and talismans we seek to move beyond the physical and into the unseen world where the astral double or spiritual counterpart (and thus true power) of the object dwells. As Dion Fortune advises, the ultimate power of any sacred object lies in the ability of the bearer to connect his or her consciousness to its representative spiritual power behind the veils. Unless we have strongly and clearly formed an alliance with the spiritual power that lies behind the object in our possession, our talismans can impart little benefit on our behalf.

To fashion a talisman of your own, begin by assessing the protective partnerships that you have already formed according to your particular religion or spiritual tradition. Nearly all religious and spiritual traditions include particular means of discernment and protection in the form of prayers, deities or symbols. Consistency within your chosen tradition or religion is important for it keeps the incoming and outgoing spiri-

---

[64] Fortune, Dion. *Glastonbury Avalon of the Heart*, Weiser Books, Boston, MA/York Beach, ME, 2000, p 93.

tual channels clear. As such, your protective partnership may include, the powers of the Name in which your *Central Flame* statement is dedicated, your guardian or an Archangelic spiritual force. Once you have found the spiritual being or quality with which you wish to align in the form of a talisman, it is wise to enter into meditation to discern the form this being or energy wishes to take. Physical forms of protective talismans are not decided upon by the bearer, they are communicated by the unseen worlds. It is our job as the bearer to listen to and discover the way in which our protective allies wish to be represented in the physical world (e.g. amulet, figurine, herb bundle, stone, etc.). With little effort, the meditative forms used to determine *The Central Flame* statement and welcome our guardian can be modified for this purpose. With discovery meditations such as this, the key is to avoid any desire to overlay our wishes or desires onto the working; instead we must allow the spiritual forces to offer their guidance into our empty and receptive vessel of consciousness. When the form of your talisman has been clearly communicated, it is time to gather the necessary items for its construction. Do not be surprised if in your meditation you are told the construction process is to take place on a certain day or at a certain time. Though the particular ways and means will vary from person to person and tradition to tradition, many talismanic creations involve a close correspondence with a place, the time of day or a celestial event. In whatever form they come, follow the instructions for the construction of your talisman to the letter.

Once your talisman is made, there are a few other operations to follow. First, listen to and learn exactly how your talisman is to be used as a protective ally. In addition, learn where and how it is to be stored when not in use. Further, it is important to remember talismans are specific to an individual. Even if you mean well, it is not appropriate for you to offer the particular powers of your talisman to another person, place or thing. Further, it is not appropriate to speak of or boast about the protective powers imbued in your talisman; desires such as these indicate an immature ego attachment to our spiritual work which will ultimately drain our true power. Lastly, well made talismans are meant to house spiritual beings and energies for the useful life of the talisman. If you carelessly misplace or lose your talisman, it is wise to perform a ritual to release the beings and energies it houses back into the natural reclamation cycles of Heaven and

Earth. Sometimes the loss of a talisman has nothing to do with our personal carelessness; the particular spiritual powers are simply through working with us. If this is the case, it is up to us to meditate to discover the form and alignment of the next talisman willing to walk with us.

Currently, I carry with me a talisman that is dedicated to the protective powers of the Celtic Goddess, Brigit. When I am not traveling it rests upon the altar in my home that is dedicated to her healing and protective abilities. When I travel, I keep this piece in a bag specially made to house and protect its spiritual imprints. Most of the time, my guardian keeps me safe and out of spiritual mischief when I am out and about in the world at large. However, once while traveling out of state, I found myself in need of the additional assistance of my talisman. I was in a foreign environment and in need of direct spiritual clarity and guidance concerning a personal matter of some urgency. Immediately upon engaging with my talisman, I felt the strength and power of Brigit's presence. I was taken into a deep meditation and shown exactly what to do. Upon exiting the meditation, I realized that not only did I have a clear direction in which to proceed, the fear and anxiety I felt prior to the meditation had lifted as well. Receipt of clear direction with a commensurate easing of fear and anxiety (which often entices us into disempowering thought-forms) is the benefit one can expect from long term talismanic work.

Spiritual Discernment in Caring for New Personal Items

We have just discussed the ways in which we can care for our physical body system when venturing beyond our homes. I would now like to discuss the manner in which we can care for the same upon purchasing new household and personal items. Just as negative/retarding energies and beings can linger in physical spaces or places, they can cling to physical items and objects. If for instance, when we shop in a street fare or used furniture store the trinkets, books and household items of our interest may (and very often do) retain an uncleansed, energetic imprint of their prior owner and/or use. Before we consider purchasing items presented in venues such as these, we should take the time to feel into their resonance. If we feel the object has an unhealthy residual imprint, we should take precaution to clear the item before placing it in our home. Even if your newly acquired item or object seems clean, you may still wish to perform a simple purification as a matter of course. As a man or woman of spirit, when we shop for new home or personal items, we should consider: 1) attending to the subtle messages of our physical body system in response to the item or object and 2) allowing time to perform a simple clearing of the object when we return home. The old adage is always true: "An ounce of prevention is worth a pound of cure." It makes good sense to take the time to set up a "new items" purification routine that is readily available and easy to incorporate into your daily life.

I tend to cleanse all new objects and articles I bring into my home if purchased second hand. I have even on occasion felt the need to cleanse new, full priced items. When I purchase a new object that feels recognizably imprinted or unhealthy, I have found it best to keep the item wrapped in the paper bag it came in when purchased, which can be burned later. Once home, I release the item from its containment and leave it outside for twenty-four hours if it is appropriate to do so. If you live where it is sunny for consistent periods of time, let the item sit in the sun for a period of twenty-four to forty-eight hours. The ultraviolet radiation of the sun is a marvelous multi-level cleanser. If I do not have long periods of reliable sun or due to its delicacy the item should not be exposed in this manner, I will instead use a good smudge, salt water or both to clear the item. Most often, I perform my new item clearing rituals outside as opposed to inside my home for obvious reasons.

Ceremony and Ritual for Spiritual Discernment

In Webster's New Collegiate Dictionary [65], the word ritual is defined as, "the established form of religious ceremony or any formal or customarily repeated act or series of acts." The word ceremony is defined as, "a formal act or series of acts prescribed by ritual." According to these dictionary definitions, a ritual is a ceremony and a ceremony is a ritual. These definitions may indeed represent the official classification of the terms; however to a practitioner of these art forms Webster's definitions are incomplete. In his book *Ritual: Power, Healing and Community*, Malidoma Patrice Somé differentiates ritual from ceremony in the following manner:

---

[65] *Webster's Seventh New Collegiate Dictionary*, G. & C. Merriam Company, Springfield, MA. 1965.

There is ritual each time a spirit is called to intervene in human affairs. The structure of the ritual is what I would like to call ceremony because it can vary from time to time and place to place. So a ceremony, perhaps, is the anatomy of a ritual. It shows what actually is taking place in the visible world, on the surface, and can therefore be seen, observed, corrected. The invisible part of the ritual, that actually happens as a result of the ceremony, is what carries the ritual quality within itself. [66]

– M. P. Somé

To summarize, the visible actions we perform consist of the ceremony; the response from the unseen worlds and the mutual communion that follows creates a ritual. Ceremony consists of the physical components of the rite: the altar, the clothing, our incantations and outward actions. A ceremony becomes a ritual when our own sincere emotional and spiritual engagement allows beings and energies of the seen and unseen worlds to come nearer to and commune with us for the greater good. Whether we are speaking of the outward gestures or the inner engagement, all ceremony and ritual must first be created upon the foundation of our own clear and sincere intention. As has been stated previously, intention is the "why" that accompanies the "what" of each ceremonial action; it is the means through which the mundane becomes the sacred.

Ceremony and ritual are vehicles of transformation within which human beings, spiritual forces and planetary energies can work together to manifest sacred intention, as condoned by the greater good. I have been performing and teaching ceremonial and ritual arts for over twelve years now in The StarHouse. In this capacity, I tell my students, "we don't *do* ritual...ritual does us." When we engage in ceremony and ritual, things change. Matter and energy are transformed and seeds are planted for new and particular growth. Ritual has the ability to influence us on all levels; thus we should never enter into a ceremonial engagement lightly or naively. When, through clear intention and purpose, we sincerely engage the will forces of our physical body, the thinking forces of our mental ability and the emotional forces of our sensing body to commune with the beings and en-

---

[66] Somé, Malidoma Patrice. *Ritual: Power, Healing and Community*, Swan/Raven & Company, Portland Oregon. 1993 p50.

ergies of the unseen worlds, matter and energy is transformed. That said, it is important to state that for the most part ritual does not thoroughly and immediately transform our entire being overnight. Because we are partially composed of the dense matter of our physical body, instantaneous transformation would be too disruptive. What you will find is that a ritual creates a seed of transformation that begins its cycle of growth and change within you. This pace is controlled by your own Higher Self and the benevolent spiritual forces you have asked to assist you. Together they gradually transform the physical body and habit body[67] to integrate the spiritual changes created by the ritual. With this general clarity regarding ceremony and ritual in mind, let us move on to discuss the specific ritual mass and banishment rites often referenced in spiritual discernment work.

In the context of spiritual discernment, personal rituals of transformation are usually focused upon the liberation from our own negative/retarding beings and energies, acquiring spiritual assistance with hardship or improving our alignment with our own higher faculties. Though largely personal at first blush, any positive transformation we sustain will augment our ability to perform the work of our soul. As such personal rituals should be directed toward serving the greater, as well as our personal, good. In the same spiritual discernment context, we may also perform transpersonal rituals through which we seek to jointly influence the transformation of the general ills such as the healing of war, famine relief, regeneration of the wetlands, an end to child abuse and the like. When engaged in transpersonal work, we lend our emotional, mental and physical energies to the reversal of the patterns of disease in the world at large. In so doing, we must always remember never to affect the free will of another human being in any way. As we have already learned, manifestations of disease, illness, hatred and hopelessness generate and are fed by particular patterned forces. To stay active, these manifestations need to feed upon that which sustains

---

[67] "Habit body" is a term we use in PCA to represent the aspect of our being that is overly attached to the familiar, the known and the predictable. It is often rooted in the comfort of routine no matter how beneficial or negative the routine's ultimate effect actually is. When we engage in ceremony and ritual we plant seeds for new habits and patterns, but first our greater intelligence is employed in identifying and unplugging our habit body's attachment to the old way lodged within our physical body system.

them. When we offer alternative patterns like healing, love, vitality and hope into the field of manifested form, we degrade the established pattern. That said, it is important to understand that just like funds we contribute to third world charities, oftentimes the energies generated in our transformational ceremonies and rituals do not actually find their intended mark. The unseen world is more complex than the average ceremonial handbook would have us believe. As men and women of spirit we will learn how to offer the energy of our transpersonal rituals over or under the forms and forces of chaos that can absorb the force of our healing prayers and ritual actions before they reach their intended destination. In the current context, it will suffice to say that transpersonal rituals created with an intention to shift global patterns of disease are best offered into the capable hands of the Archangelic forces.

Through our practical pursuits in the context of spiritual discernment, we will undoubtedly become familiar with the terms ritual mass and banishment rites. What do these terms really mean and why are they important to those of us interested in developing a practice of spiritual discernment? In contemporary religious terms, a ritual mass consists of a sequence of particular prayers and ceremonies forming the Eucharistic rite which celebrates spiritual communion with God. In transdenominational terms, a ritual mass is a ceremonial act performed in alignment with the creative powers and spiritual forces of Heaven and Earth to which you offer your supreme veneration. Within this ceremony one may request a blessing and support from the benevolent beings of the unseen worlds toward a specific personal or transpersonal transformation of matter and/ or energy. A banishment rite is a specific type of ceremony that consecrates a particular act of spiritual discernment in our life. In banishment rites our focus is on releasing, ending or severing a prior path, connection or affiliation on both the physical and metaphysical level. In simple terms a ceremony done to consecrate your *Central Flame* is a "yes" ceremony; a banishment rite is a "no" ceremony. A ritual mass is a form and a banishment rite defines the terms of the form. If you like, think of the ritual mass as a cake and the banishment rite as the flavor of the batter and icing.

If you choose to pick up any of the reference materials cited in this book (and I sincerely hope you do) you will notice that several of these sources contain ritual masses and banishment rites written by their authors in an effort to provide an example of the kind of ceremony that can be used to banish negative/retarding spiritual beings and energies. You will undoubtedly notice that I have not placed any such rites within the pages of this book. As stated initially in this section, for a rite to work it has to fully engage you physically and emotionally before it can become an effective tool for personal transformation. Further, it must be created and performed in deference to the spiritual forces to whom you pay your supreme veneration. Some of the incantations and rites you will find in books written by Dion Fortune, W.G. Gray, R.J. Stewart and Caitlin Matthews in particular are quite powerful and helpful in a spiritual discernment context. Though the rites in books written by another experienced occultist can provide a solid foundation for us when we are working to determine the components of our own ritual mass or banishment rite, we should not use another person's ritual form if we are in no way physically, emotionally or spiritually related to the person or their path. If you are well rooted in the arts and disciplines of the Western Esoteric Tradition, many of the aforementioned adept's work may suit your needs perfectly. If not, they will likely not serve you.

Rather than including a ritual mass or banishment rite of my own, as might be expected of me, I am choosing to do something different. Having created, performed and taught ceremony and ritual for nearly twelve years, I could certainly compose a ceremony like those we are used to seeing in esoteric texts. However, I truly feel this would be of little value. In keeping with my own beliefs, I would much rather encourage you to spend the time required to determine your own needs, write your own ceremony and perform your own ritual. Throughout this book there are several seed exercises that you can piece together into quite a powerful personal ritual mass or banishment rite for these purposes. I know that when you do so, this ceremony will be far better suited to your needs than anything I could otherwise compose on your behalf.

What To Do When It All Fails?

(We all exist within) the power of the Divine in Whom you live and move and have your being and of Whom you are a part.

So you need never worry about the powers of darkness. All the same, don't get into positions where they are liable to bite you. If they do, see to it that you bite back, that you conquer the thing. [68]– *W.E. Butler*

Because we are soul-based human beings seeking the experience of an Earth life and all that it entails, part of our learning comes from the wallops born of our own foibles. We are designed to fail from time to time in faithfully and successfully executing our spiritual discernment practices. Sometimes we will fail because we forget what we know or become complacent. In these instances, we will receive a timely "whack" which instructs us to collect ourselves in remembrance of our responsibilities as men and women of spirit. Other times we will fail because we come upon a being or energy that we have not previously encountered, though its sophistication eventually thrusts us to new levels of awareness and ability, upon our first meeting we absorb the "whack" that teaches us something new. Finally, on occasion we will encounter negative/retarding energies that our being must experience so that we learn to let go or leave a situation that we should not be in. Whether by forgetfulness, unfamiliarity or redirection when we take a spiritual hit we must, as W. E. Butler puts it, "bite back." This does not imply that we engage in a long and grueling battle with the beings and energies we've encountered; it means we employ our will to stand up, break the connection between us and them, brush ourselves off and move on! Sometimes we can accomplish this recovery alone and other times we will need to employ the advice or services of a friend who is proficiently skilled in these matters. To begin with, let us speak to that which we can and should do for ourselves in the event that we absorb an otherworldly blow.

If you recall Dion Fortune's earlier instruction, negative/ retarding beings and energies can only affect us if we have an access point or trigger waiting to be touched within our physical body system. As we have discussed, these access points are a function of our own unhealed fears, wounds, physical weak spots, ancestral ties and cellular memories. Most often blows offered by malevolent otherworldly energies or beings occur when our defenses are underemployed: when we are sleeping, resting

---

[68] Butler, W.E. *Lords of Light: The Path of Initiation in the Western Tradition*, Destiny Books, Rochester Vermont, 1990, pp. 61-62.

or engaged in something so fully that our discerning mind is truly elsewhere. Suddenly we rouse ourselves to the realization that we have become the unwary victim of an unhealthy parasitic invasion. Because we have already discussed the symptoms and signals of spiritual distress I will not repeat them here but instead refer you back to the prior section if you do not immediately recall how these invasions impact the physical body system. When you have taken a hit, what do you do next?

Unless you feel strong enough to fight the entity or energy you are encountering (and I would not advise anyone do this in a weakened state) you must instead strive to break the direct connection between the parasitic being or energy and yourself by finding your way to a different environment as quickly as possible. If you are dealing with a dream-induced invasion in your own home, get out of bed and go to your altar. If you are dealing with a dream-induced invasion while staying in a hotel, rise from sleep, take a shower and leave the room for a while, taking a walk to a park or natural setting near by. If you are smack in the middle of a 16th century battlefield on a tour with forty people who are not leaving for another hour, sit down or stand, call to your guardian, form and invoke a protective sphere around you, speak your *Central Flame* statement (softly, yet aloud) and call upon Archangelic forces for help. First and foremost, you must remove yourself from the negative/retarding spiritual being's or energy's field of influence by breaking the connection as quickly as possible.

Once you have broken the connection and found yourself firmly rooted in the embrace of the spiritual forces that assist you, you should focus on rebuilding the vitality of your physical body system. Drinking fluids such as water infused with Bach's Five-Flower Remedy, lemon juice or vitamins and minerals is an excellent first step. From here, it is important to perform a personal purification rite. Often a salt bath or salt and olive oil scrub in the shower works quite well. After your purification rite is complete, eat a meal of grounded and nourishing foods that strengthen your connection to the vital, creative forces of the Earth. Finally, it can be helpful to contact a spiritual elder or colleague who you trust to request their assistance in checking for any remnants of the unhealthy otherworldly connection that may remain.

Once out of the crisis mode, it is important to engage in an act of physical body system repair such that the portal that invited the attack is sealed, thus thwarting future invasions. We begin this process by looking deep inside ourselves to find where the portal exists within our physical body system. To do this, we must call up the particulars of the invasion as well as the corresponding forms of our fears, loathing or wounds. From here we must clear the fear, hatred or pain and seal the doors of our vital body against such frequencies. I will give you an example from my own spiritual life, which I hope will help to explain the steps in this recovery process in more detail. This methodology combines three of the techniques referenced earlier in the text and thus serves nicely as the culminating exercise of this book.

One morning after a particularly draining night fighting off an invasion, I pushed myself awake through the deep throws of a nightmare. In the dream I was among a group of people who were fighting soldiers away from the heavy, wooden doors of a great temple. The soldiers were breaking through and I was desperate in my knowing that, after hours of defending ourselves against their attack, we were no longer able to hold them back. I also knew we would all be killed once the doors were forced open. Fear of spiritual failure and a tortured death was the trigger point that this particular parasitic being found alive and vulnerable within me and thus exploited in the dream. After waking, I forced myself out of bed and immediately took a salt scrub shower to stimulate my circulation and shift the dream-induced energy currents coursing through my body. From here I got a cup of hot herbal tea and went to my altar. In the embrace of a sacred sphere and in the presence of my guardian, I recalled up the images from the dream. Then I spoke my intention to identify and heal this entry point within my physical body system that created a hospitable place for fear of spiritual failure. As in *The Body Barometer* exercise, I scanned my physical body system to determine where the physical and psychic trigger for this invasion lay within me. In that moment, a distant cellular memory came to the forefront of my sacred imagination. In the scenes that followed, I recalled a memory within which I was unable to protect a circle of women from a group of religious zealots; in the end we all died a torturous and humiliating death. Of course this memory was shocking and very emotional as these recollections and discoveries often are. Once I identified the psychic entry point as the memory of attack, I asked the intelligence within my physical body system to show me the physi-

195

cal dwelling place of this cellular memory. I was informed this memory was lodged within the walls of my heart. Now I knew both the psychic and physical entry point and was thus ready to proceed. From here I used the same method employed to remove unlawful images to lift this psychic and physical entry out of my physical body system and close the point of entry.

However difficult the discovery of our triggers and portals to parasitic invasion may be, we must not become lost in the recollection of our own fears and wounding. If we do, we will stay vulnerable to future provocation. When we invoke a memory, fear or wound we must keep our reactions in check so that we don't end up lost in the pain and anguish of our memory's affinity for the subject matter at hand. We must instead journalistically identify the memory's contents and then release our attachment to it. Again, the steps in this process are 1) get out of the cycle and break the connection, 2) shift the physical body system's energy field, 3) fortify the physical body system, and 4) perform the spiritual work necessary to fully recover from the attack and prevent the likelihood of similar future attacks.

When things fall apart, as undoubtedly they will from time to time in our spiritual discernment work, we must never, never succumb to the victim's logic that would like to convince us that it is all too hard, we will not recover and nothing we do is good enough. I know from experience just how enticing these thoughts can become. I also know how wonderful it feels when, due to our own good preparatory efforts, we successfully circumvent the harmful intentions of an unhealthy otherworldly being or energy. Finally, I am one hundred percent convinced that no matter how bad it gets, there is always an unseen ally waiting on the other side of the veils to meet our extended hand in partnership toward restoration. Often there are human allies standing by in the same capacity. Men and women of spirit are never alone in these endeavors. So do not let yourself get away with the victim's logic that would convince you otherwise and keep you mired in a web of spiritual confusion and impotence. When we come to a difficult crossroads in our spiritual and magical practice, we must stand up, brush ourselves off and reaffirm that all that is sacred to us is still within us to be tapped and redeployed. The only error is in lying down, giving up and waving the white flag of surrender.

Conclusion

This book set forth to change a term of art and thus a mind-set among esoteric practitioners. At its conclusion I would like to offer these thoughts. Though many principles pertinent to the unseen worlds remain consistent through time, other principles change and evolve just as humanity, technology, consciousness, the Earth and the Universe changes and evolves. As spiritual practitioners our duty is threefold. We must study the works of our spiritual ancestors in reverence to their achievements. From here we must assess the ways in which our life and times necessitates changes and/or adjustments to these works. Finally, we must focus the results of our work on the future generations and the greater good to which we've all aspired. Through this book I have endeavored to honor this threefold duty. And, as I imagine my spiritual ancestors did, I am interested to discover the subsequent work that will undoubtedly come forth to augment this topic in the future. That said it is also my hope that this book will assist earnest practitioners to create and maintain their own spiritual discernment practices in reverence to the foundations of the past, the relevant changes for today and the greater future good they too endeavor to serve.

Bibliography

Beyond Words Publishing, *Messages from Water*, Hillsboro Oregon 2004, Written by Dr. Masaru Emoto Translated by David Thayne, 2004.

Burns, David D., Dr. *Feeling Good: The New Moon Therapy*, Avon Books: An Imprint of HarperCollins Publishers, New York, NY, 1980.

Bond, Frederick Bligh, *The Gate of Remembrance,* Collector's Library of the Unknown, Time-Life Books, Alexandria VA; originally published by B.H. Blackwell, Broad Street, Oxford UK, 1918.

W. E. Butler, *Apprenticed to Magic: The Path to Magical Attainment.* Thoth Publications, Loughborough, Leicestershire, UK, 2002.

Butler, W.E., *Lords of Light: The Path of Initiation in the Western Mysteries*, Destiny Books, Rochester Vermont, 1990.

Cornford, Francis M., *Plato's Cosmology The Timaeus of Plato*, Hackett Publishing Company. Indianapolis/Cambridge, Indiana, 1997.

Dunselman, Ron, *In Place of the Self: How Drugs Work*, Hawthorn Press, 1995.

Fortune, Dion, *Glastonbury Avalon of the Heart*, Weiser Books, Boston, MA/York Beach, ME, 2000.

Fortune, Dion, *Psychic Self-Defense*, Weiser Books, Boston, MA/York Beach, ME, 2001.

Fortune, Dion, *The Training and Work of an Initiate*, Weiser Books, Boston, MA/York Beach, ME, 2000.

Fortune, Dion, *Esoteric Orders and Their Work*, Samuel Weiser, Inc., York Beach, ME, 2000.

Fortune, Dion, *Dion Fortune's Book of the Dead*, Weiser Books, Boston, MA/York Beach, ME, 2005.

Fortune, Dion, *The Cosmic Doctrine*, Weiser Books, Boston, MA/York Beach, ME, 2000

Gray, William G., *Exorcising the Tree of Evil*, Kima Global Publishers, Cape Town South Africa, 2002.

Grieve, Mrs. M., *A Modern Herbal: The Medicinal, Culinary, Cosmetic and Economic Properties, Cultivation and Folk-Lore of Herbs, Grasses, Fungi, Shrubs and Trees with Their Modern Scientific Uses*, Dover Publication, 1981.

Hall, Manly P., *Paracelsus: His Mystical and Medical Philosophy*, Philosophical Research Society, Los Angeles, California, 1997.

Knight, Gareth, From the Forward to *Esoteric Orders and their Work*, by Dion Fortune.

MacEowen, Frank, *The Spiral of Memory and Belonging: A Celtic Path of Soul and Kinship*, New World Library, Novato California, 2004.

MacLeod, Fiona, *The Immortal Hour*, Thomas B. Mosher, Portland Maine, 1907.

Matthews, Caitlín, *The Psychic Protection Handbook*, Piatkus Books Ltd, London, Great Britain, 2005.

Prather, Hugh, *Notes to Myself*, Real People Press, Moab, Utah, 1970.

Prokofieff, Sergei O., *The Heavenly Sophia and the Being Anthroposophia*, Temple Lodge Publishing, 1996.

Scupoli, Lorenzo, *Unseen Warfare: the Spirital Combat and Path to Paradise of Lorenzo Scupoli edited by Nicodemus of the Holy Mountain and revised by Theophan the Recluse*, St. Vladimir's Seminary Press, New York, 1978.

Shaw, Gregory, *Theurgy and the Soul: The Neoplatonism of Iamblichus*, Pennsylvania State University Press, University Park, Pennsylvania, 1951.

Somé, Malidoma Patrice, *Ritual: Power, Healing and Community*, Swan/Raven & Company, Portland Oregon, 1993.

Steiner, Rudolph, *True and False Spiritual Paths*, Rudolph Steiner Press, Dornach Switzerland, Third Edition, 1985.

Steiner, Rudolph, *Knowledge of the Higher Worlds and its Attainment*, Anthroposophic Press, Inc. New York, 1947.

Steiner, Rudolph, *The Forming of Destiny and Life after Death*, Lecture 4: The connection between the spiritual and the physical worlds and how they are experienced after death. December 7th 1915. Rudolph Steiner Archives, www.rsarchive.org.

Steiner, Rudolph, *The Spiritual Hierarchies and the Physical World Reality and Illusion*, Anthroposophic Press, Inc. New York, 1996.

Thorsson, Edred, *Futhark: A Handbook of Rune Magic*, Samuel Weiser, 1984.

Tisserand, Robert, *The Art of Aromatherapy*, Healing Arts Press, Rochester, VT, 1977.

Webster's Seventh New Collegiate Dictionary, G. & C. Merriam Company, Springfield, Massachusetts, 1965.

Young, N.D, D. Gary, *Aromatherapy: The Essential Beginning*, Essential Press Publishing, Salt Lake City, UT, 1995.

Seedbearers - 36-50
115 - 137

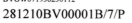
CPSIA information can be obtained at www.ICGtesting.com
Printed in the USA
BVOW071936230112

281210BV00001B/7/P